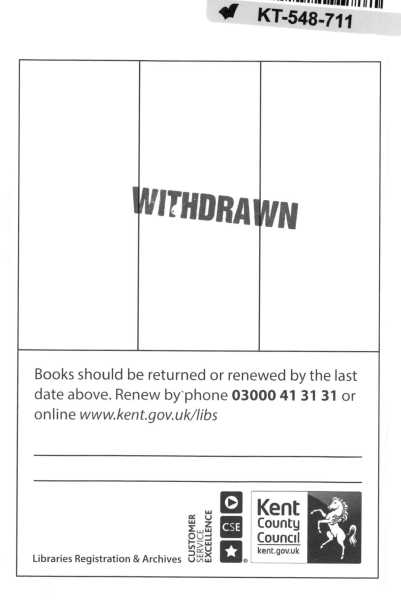

THE BUSINESS OF SLEEP

THE BUSINESS OF SLEEP

How Sleeping Better Can Transform Your Career

VICKI CULPIN

BLOOMSBURY BUSINESS

LONDON · NEW YORK · OXFORD · NEW DELHI · SYDNEY

BLOOMSBURY BUSINESS
Bloomsbury Publishing Plc
50 Bedford Square, London, WC1B 3DP, UK

BLOOMSBURY, BLOOMSBURY BUSINESS and the Diana logo are trademarks
of Bloomsbury Publishing Plc

First published in Great Britain 2018

Cover design by danileighdesign.com
Cover images © iStock

A catalogue record for this book is available from the British Library.

Library of Congress Cataloging-in-Publication Data
Names: Culpin, Vicki, 1971- author.
Title: The business of sleep : how sleeping better can transform
your career / by Vicki Culpin.
Description: London, UK ; New York, NY, USA : Bloomsbury Business,
an imprint of Bloomsbury Publishing, Plc, 2018. |
Includes bibliographical references and index.
Identifiers: LCCN 2017053925 | ISBN 9781472936578 (hb) |
ISBN 9781472936585 (epdf) | ISBN 9781472936592 (exml)
Subjects: LCSH: Sleep–Popular works. | Career development.
Classification: LCC RA786 .C855 2018 | DDC 613.7/94–dc23
LC record available at https://lccn.loc.gov/2017053925

ISBN: HB: 978-1-4729-3657-8
        ePDF: 978-1-4729-3658-5
        eBook: 978-1-4729-3660-8

Typeset by Integra Software Services Pvt. Ltd.
Printed and bound in Great Britain

To find out more about our authors and books visit www.bloomsbury.com and
sign up for our newsletters.

For Marie -- I am the Luckiest

CONTENTS

ACKNOWLEDGEMENTS

I have been working with individuals across a variety of industries and geographies for many years, and every time I talk about resilience and sleep I learn a little bit more – a little bit more about how poor sleep affects an individual's ability to do their job, a little bit more about how organizational culture continues to perpetuate the myth that presenteeism and productivity are the same thing, a little bit more about how teams and departments are driven to do more with less, and work longer and harder under increasing pressure, and a little bit more about the resilience of the human body and human spirit.

For me, and the job that I do, every day is a school day, every day I learn, and I owe a huge debt to all of you participants on short courses, and students on degree programmes, that have shared your experiences with me, often in very frank and candid ways. I am frequently humbled by your honesty and your authenticity – this book would not have happened without you.

I would also like to thank all of my colleagues at Ashridge Executive Education, who send me press clippings, blogs, research and articles every time sleep is mentioned. You are my collective research team, and your support is truly wonderful.

It is important to say a big thank you to my family and friends, who provide the fun, the laughter and the emotional support, making sure I always sleep well.

Finally, to Marie – as my co-pilot, we have been working together on this project for a long time. You worked tirelessly alongside me for months and months; you listened to me drone on about the latest sleep research, and endlessly supported me, cajoled me and encouraged me from the start to the end. Without you I would not have started this journey and without you I would not have finished it. I can't wait to move on to our next journey together, whatever that may be.

Introduction:
The wake-up call

'It was the best of times, it was the worst of times.' Perhaps not the most original opening given that some guy called Charles Dickens used this to start his book *The Tale of Two Cities* almost 160 years ago (1), but a phrase that is as pertinent today in the world of organizational well-being as it was for Dickens in 1850's Paris and London. Never before has there been so much research focused on the topic of sleep; why sleep is needed, how sleep works and the consequences of poor sleep on both the body and mind. Never before have we been in a position to use brain scanning advances such as magnetic resonance imagery (MRI), to enable researchers to 'see' how sleep affects our thought processes, and never before have we had access to big data that allows us to understand the impact of poor sleep on organizational, national and global scales. And yet, according to some quite significant and impactful pieces of large-scale research, never before have significant percentages of working adults been so sleep deprived.[1] The Centers for Disease Control and Prevention in the United States found that more than one-third of American adults were regularly getting too little sleep (Liu et al., 2104 in RAND), a figure that led them to announce that insufficient sleep was a 'public health problem' (2), and in a 2013 study by the National Sleep Foundation (3), they reported the percentage of adults' sleep patterns:

	US	UK	Japan	Germany	Canada
Less than 6 hours' sleep per night	18%	16%	16%	9%	6%
6–7 hours' sleep per night	27%	19%	40%	21%	20%
Total % of adults getting less than 7 hours' **sleep per night**	**45%**	**35%**	**56%**	**30%**	**26%**

Source: https://sleepfoundation.org/sleep-polls-data/other-polls/2013-international-bedroom-poll.

Given that the National Sleep Foundation (3), the American Academy of Sleep Medicine and the Sleep Research Society (4) all recommend that adults between the ages of 18 and 60 **should sleep for at least 7 hours per night,** over half of Japanese adults are not getting enough sleep, and nearly half of US and UK adults are in a similar position.

Most of us are familiar with the start of *A Tale of Two Cities*, but do you know what comes next? 'It was the age of enlightenment, it was the age of foolishness.' And again, never has a truer word been spoken in relation to the world of sleep research and the impact on both business performance and organizational well-being. It really is the age of enlightenment – you only need to use the search terms 'impact of poor sleep' on the internet[2] to read well-researched articles, by reliable sources such as the NHS, the Mayo Clinic, the National Sleep Society and the American Sleep Society, explaining the consequences of poor sleep, which include poorer memory, attention, decision-making and creativity in the short term, and seven of the top fifteen leading causes of death (in the United States) in the longer term, such as cardiovascular disease, accidents, diabetes and hypertension (5). Yet, despite the access to leading research, explaining the serious cognitive and health consequences of insufficient or poor quality sleep, despite high-profile CEOs leaving office or taking long-term sick leave because of fatigue and burn-out, despite the addition of sleep hygiene courses in corporate well-being and occupational health packages, and despite increased news and media coverage on the dangers of being sleepy, it is still the age of foolishness if nearly half of the UK and US adult populations are not getting enough sleep.

Such are the dangers of poor sleep that the *Guinness Book of World Records* will no longer ratify a world record attempt at sleep deprivation,[3] although feel free to try and break the world record for the number of hamburgers eaten in 3 minutes (12 hamburgers), or the number of jalapeno chilli peppers eaten in 1 minute (16 jalapeno peppers)! Sleep is so important to human survival that whilst the exact mechanisms are still not known, continuous sleep deprivation will eventually lead to death. However, dying from sleep deprivation will not happen to a healthy human being for one fundamental reason – the body (or the brain) will not allow it. This is a really critical point, and one that emphasizes the importance of sleep to human health and functioning. An individual can actively 'choose' not to eat, and will eventually starve to death. She can decide not to take in any fluids, and will, after a much shorter period of time, die from dehydration. During starvation or dehydration, the body will resort to desperate attempts to 'force' an individual to consume food or water, but ultimately, the individual can decide whether to eat or drink. This will not happen for sleep. At some point, if you are sleep deprived, your body will force you to fall asleep and you will have absolutely no control over it. You might fight against it with all of your will, but, ultimately, the human body (and human brain) will win (6). While this is vital for human survival, and demonstrates how critical sleep is for functioning, it also flags up some of the inherent dangers of sleep deprivation, and explains why so many vehicle accidents and fatalities are a result of sleepy driving or falling asleep at the wheel.

The business case

There are three ways of examining the consequences of poor sleep, all of which are interlinked. Not getting enough sleep (sleep quantity), or not the right type of sleep (sleep quality), affects people at the individual level, with physical, social, emotional and cognitive consequences (covered in this book). These in turn, manifest themselves in behaviour which 'show up' in both personal and organizational life (such as cyber-loafing (7), experience of line manager abusive supervision (8) and leader–follower relationships (9), decreased organizational citizenship behaviour (10) and increased unethical behaviour at work (11)), resulting in performance and productivity decrements which can be generalized to industry sectors or to national economies.

In 2016, RAND Europe published a study where they examined the economic cost of insufficient sleep. From their data and computational

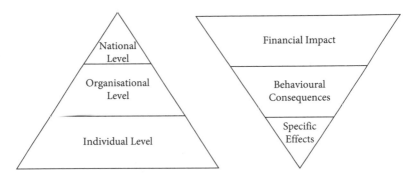

FIGURE I.1 *The relationship between level of analysis and impact of poor sleep.*

modelling, three shocking facts (at the individual, organizational and national levels) emerged (12):

- Individuals who sleep on average for less than 6 hours per night have a 13 per cent higher mortality risk than an individual sleeping between 7 and 9 hours per night, and those that sleep between 6 and 7 hours per night have a 7 per cent increase in their mortality risk.

- On an annual basis, the UK loses 0.2 million working days a year due to insufficient sleep, and the United States loses 1.23 million working days.[4]

- These increased mortality rates and lower productivity levels (as a result of absenteeism) cost the UK economy between $36.7 billion and $50 billion per year, and cost the United States between $280.6 billion and $411 billion per year.

The case for taking poor sleep seriously does not get any starker, or any clearer than this. Getting the right amount of sleep each and every night can reduce mortality, improve organizational effectiveness and save the UK economy between $36.7 billion and $50 billion (1.36–1.86 per cent of GDP) every year.

It is the age of enlightenment – the figures speak for themselves; let this not be the age of foolishness.

Structure of the book

By describing first, how sleep works; secondly, what the consequences of poor sleep are; and, finally, what can be done about it, this book provides the business case for taking this issue seriously (Part One – The Consequences of Poor Sleep), and the help and guidance on making small, yet significant, changes to improve both your sleep quality and your sleep quantity (Part Two – The Causes and Solutions for Poor Sleep). If you need further convincing that inadequate sleep is a real issue, start with Part One, the consequences of poor sleep. Here, I focus on the effects of poor sleep at the individual level – cognitive, social and emotional and physical effects that are particularly pertinent to individuals within a working environment. These include poorer memory and attention, poor decision-making, a reduction in creativity and innovation, poorer physical health and reduced mood. Given that some clever chap called Goethe[5] noted that 'knowing is not enough, we must apply, willing is not enough, we must do' (14), Part Two of the book focuses on the causes of reduced sleep so that we can look at what can be done to improve it, whether they be environmental (technology, noise, temperature), psychological or physiological (caffeine, alcohol, exercise, shift work or jet lag) factors.

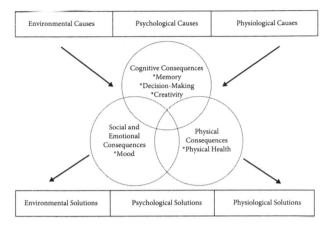

FIGURE I.2 *The causes and consequences of poor sleep.*

How much sleep do we need?

Sleep is hugely individual; that is, what is right for one person may be too much or too little for another. This is important, because your sleep need is determined by a whole range of factors individual to you, including your age, health and, to some extent, gender (e.g. pregnant women and post-partum women have different sleep needs). Yet, this variability across sleep need does not vary as much as you might think (or wish it did), and is not an excuse for not getting enough sleep. If you wake up in the morning, and the majority of the time you do not feel fully rested, then this is a sign that you are not getting enough sleep, and/or that your sleep is of poor quality. This test may be crude, but it is a remarkably effective way of listening to your body's sleep needs.[6] If you are getting the right amount and the right quality sleep that you need, each and every night, you should be waking up every morning (give yourself 5 minutes to gain full alertness) feeling refreshed and rested. Whilst there are fluctuations across the day in terms of how alert you might feel (such as the post-lunch 'dip'), you should generally be able to manage a full day without a nap, or without falling asleep on the sofa before dinner. Of course, we all have bad sleep nights, and crazy schedules that keep us working late on the odd occasion, but if this 'odd occasion' becomes the norm, or it has become so much the norm that you don't even notice or think about how tired you feel, then it is worth stopping and reflecting on your sleep patterns.

In 2015, the National Sleep Foundation was one of the first organizations to officially recommend sleep time durations for all, from new-borns to older adults:

Age	Recommended (hours per night)	May be appropriate (hours per night)	Not recommended (hours per night)
New-borns (0–3 months)	14–17	11–13 and 18–19	Less than 11 More than 19
Infants (4–11 months)	12–15	10–11 and 16–18	Less than 10 More than 18
Toddlers (1–2 years)	11–14	9–10 and 15–16	Less than 9 More than 16
Pre-schoolers (3–5 years)	10–13	8–9 and 14	Less than 8 More than 14
School-aged children (6–13 years)	9–11	7–8 and 12	Less than 7 More than 12
Teenagers (14–17 years)	8–10	7 and 11	Less than 7 More than 11
Young adults (18–25 years)	*7–9*	*6 and 10–11*	*Less than 6 More than 11*
Adults (26–64 years)	*7–9*	*6 and 10*	*Less than 6 More than 10*
Older adults (65 years +)	7–8	5–6 and 9	Less than 5 More than 9

Source: Hirshkowitz et al. National Sleep Foundation's sleep time duration recommendations: Methodology and results summary (15).

Not only is getting the right amount of sleep (quantity) important, the quality of sleep is also critical. Understanding the sleep cycle and how sleep works will illustrate why quality, or depth of sleep, is just as important as the amount of sleep you gain each night, but an analogy may also help. Chris Winter in his book *The Sleep Solution* describes the impact of poor sleep quality as that akin to an orchestra playing a symphony with a break in proceedings every 20 minutes. Whilst every note may be played with perfect technical precision, there will be little enjoyment of the piece (6). The music will be fragmented, and this, like sleep fragmentation, has as much impact on the success of the piece (or the benefit of sleep) as the fact that every note is played (every hour of sleep is gained).

How does sleep work?

Process S and Process C

As humans we have two basic sleep mechanisms. One works on a roughly 24-hour[7] cycle, and one in a linear fashion.

The linear process, often referred to as the 'drive for sleep', is determined by how much sleep we have recently had, and so is known as a sleep-dependent process (Process S). The longer we are awake, the greater the need for sleep, but once we have had sufficient sleep, the process re-sets itself and starts again. If we have had some sleep, but not enough, the 'drive for sleep' will be reduced, but will not completely disappear.

The cyclical process is not determined by sleep at all, but by our 24-hour internal circadian processes (Process C). These processes are synchronized or calibrated by external cues to time (known as zeitgebers, or 'time-givers'), with the most important being light and dark.

As an analogy, think of Process C as a ball, and Process S as a moving conveyor belt. During the day, the ball is moving along the conveyor belt, turning as it goes, and as it turns it is taking in all of the external cues to the different times of the day. As it gets dark, it gets to the end of the belt. During the day, the conveyor belt has been getting a bit steeper, because you are getting more tired, and as the ball gets to the top of the belt you have the perfect storm – the ball (Process C) tells your body it is time to sleep because core temperature has dropped, and it is dark outside, and you have been awake a long time and so you are tired (Process S) and at the end of the belt. You fall asleep. While you are asleep, the ball rolls down the conveyor belt, still turning as it goes (the circadian rhythms continue throughout the night whilst you are asleep), and when you wake up you are ready to start again.

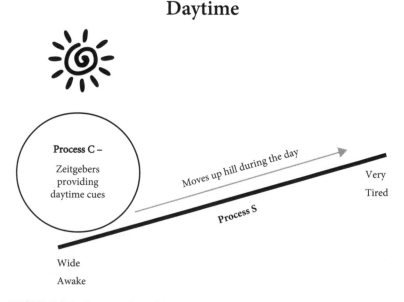

FIGURE I.3 *Process C and Process S during the day.*

Night time

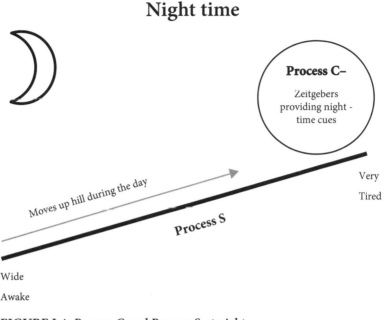

FIGURE I.4 *Process C and Process S at night.*

Sleep stages

Humans, in fact all mammals, have two distinct states of sleep – NREM (non-rapid eye movement) and REM (rapid eye movement sleep) sleep – and a variety of physiological variables, including eye movement, body movement and brain wave activity, show that these two different states are as distinct from each other as they are from being fully awake (18). NREM, or 'non-REM' sleep, itself has three stages, N1, N2 and N3,[8] with N1 and N2 the stages of sleep that we may think of as lighter sleep, and N3 as slow wave sleep (SWS) or deep sleep. During NREM sleep, we are able to move our body (especially in N1 and N2 lighter sleep), whereas in REM sleep we have what is known as muscle atonia; muscle paralysis. Given that the majority of human dreaming occurs during REM sleep, not being able to physically act out our dreams due to paralysis is certainly advantageous!

Under usual circumstances, adults will take about 15–20 minutes to go from N1 light sleep through into SWS (deep sleep), and they will then cycle through the sleep stages during the night (approximately 90 minutes per cycle), with the majority of SWS in the first half of the night, and the majority of REM sleep in the second half[9] (see diagram below), waking up from REM sleep or light sleep in the morning if able to do so naturally (it is of course a different story if you need to use an alarm). Waking up from N1 light sleep usually means you awake feeling refreshed, whereas waking in the middle of SWS, or deep sleep, can lead to grogginess and lethargy (think about waking up on the sofa on a Saturday afternoon after an 'accidental' nap).

Whilst the amount of REM and NREM sleep (at each of the different stages) does differ markedly from childhood through to adulthood, healthy adults up until the age of 60–65 years share a similar pattern in terms of time to fall asleep (known as sleep latency), how much

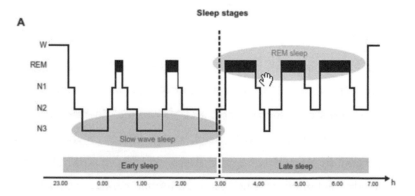

time is spent awake during the night (known as 'wake after sleep onset', or WASO) and time in each sleep stage (see diagram below).

To maintain health, and to ensure that cognitive, social and emotional functioning is not affected, both sleep quality and sleep

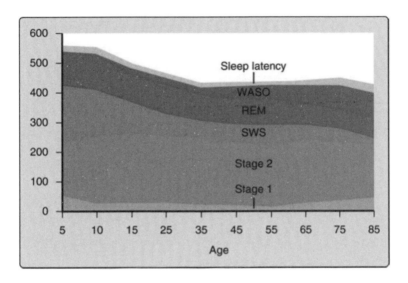

quantity are important. That is, we must move along the whole sleep process to get the right amount of sleep, but we must also move up and down the cycles to gain the right amount of the different sleep stages. In Part One of the book (consequences), we look at what happens when we don't get enough sleep (quantity) or we don't get the right type of sleep (quality), and in Part Two (causes), we examine the reasons why our quality and quantity of sleep may be affected, and what we can put in place to help improve our sleep in the future. This book should, therefore, add to your age of enlightenment, and motivate you to do something differently to improve your sleep, thus avoiding the age of foolishness.

PART ONE

The Consequences of Poor Sleep

1

Memories are made of this – sleep and memory

If you were to take a guess, how many times per day do you rely on your memory at work? Twenty or thirty times? Maybe more? And what type of things do you use your memory for during the working day, or perhaps more importantly, what types of things do you forget during the working day? Times of appointments, key facts for a report, the name of a new colleague? So, what about driving to work? Without procedural memory (memory for procedures such as driving a car or riding a bike) you wouldn't be able to remember how to drive, and in fact, without memory, you wouldn't even recall that you had a job to go to in the first place. Memory is not just a repository of facts and figures that we can draw upon when we need them (although of course it does that too), it shapes our very existence; it determines who we think we are, how we view the world (based on how we remember the past) and how we plan for the future, eloquently summarised by Steven Shapin in an article in *The New Yorker* – 'Time, reality and identity are each curated by memory' (1).

Given the critical importance of memory, not just to success in organizational life, but to our very being, it is perhaps not surprising that the effect of sleep on memory systems is one of the most well-researched areas in the sleep literature to date, with a particular increase in research activity over the past decade. However, although there has been a recent proliferation in research examining the relationship between sleep and memory, the general benefits of sleep for memory were established as early as 1885, and so the recent focus has been on examining the *types* of memory that benefit from good sleep, and *when* you should sleep for maximum advantage.

In 1885, Hermann Ebbinghaus, a professor at the University of Berlin, published a series of memory experiments, based on a sample size of one – himself! Whilst, by modern standards of scientific rigour, this may be somewhat problematic, the work of Ebbinghaus, specifically his discovery of the 'forgetting curve' (he noted that forgetting occurs very quickly within the first few hours after learning of the material to be remembered, and that after a few days, whatever is still retained, is relatively stable over time), has stood the test of time, with memory researchers today still referring to rates of forgetting demonstrated by Ebbinghaus over a century ago. To understand how memory works, Ebbinghaus gave himself lists of non-words to learn. These non-words were of a very particular nature; they were consonant, vowel, consonant tri-grams (VEK, PIV, etc.) and Ebbinghaus had spent many years committing lists of these non-words to memory, and then subsequently testing himself over different periods of time (such as immediately, an hour, a day or a month after learning). During these experiments Ebbinghaus slept as usual (although we don't know what 'as usual' looked like for him), and he noticed that his rate of forgetting was somewhat reduced when he slept between learning the words and recalling them. In 1914, the relationship between learning and sleep was again demonstrated in Germany, this time with a grand total of six participants, with learning material in the evening resulting in less forgetting even 24 hours later when compared with learning followed by wakefulness, and so the connection between memory (learning) and sleep began to take hold (2).

The message, from over 150 years of research examining the effect of sleep on learning and memory, is that good sleep improves memory. Getting a good night of sleep prior to learning new material and/or sleeping between learning the new information and needing to recall it have both been shown to improve subsequent performance. For example, in a study where individuals were sleep deprived prior to being given new material to learn, there was an incredible 40 per cent reduction in their ability to form new memories. Interestingly, when the material was divided into that with positive, neutral and negative connotations, memory was superior for the positive and negative material for those participants who had slept as normal, (not surprising given that we know that emotion aids the encoding of memories) but for those who had been sleep deprived, performance was poor on both the neutral and positive material, but *not* on the negative material. That is, although overall performance was worse for the sleep deprived individuals, this reduction was only across positive and neutral memories, the negative memories were still remembered, showing a negative bias for the memories after poor sleep (3).

So, perhaps this is where we should end this chapter – one of the central tenets for the business case of getting more sleep is that it can improve your memory, and given that memory is not just critical for organizational success (turning up late to meetings, failing to recall critical sales figures or missing a deadline are certainly career derailers), but is fundamental to an individual's core identity as a human, then getting more sleep to aid memory performance is a compelling argument. But of course, the more intellectually curious (or cynical) of us want to know more than this. Is all learning and memory improved by sleep? Does it matter when we sleep for memory improvements? What does 'good' sleep, that improves memory and learning, look like? To answer these questions, we need to understand a little more about the different stages and types of memory.

Paul Reber, Professor of Psychology at Northwestern University, Illinois, believes that if it is at all possible to liken the brain's ability to store memories to a computer hard drive, then the capacity would be in the region of several petabytes. That is, approximately 1,000,000 gigabytes, or 3 million hours of TV shows, taking 300 years to play (4). A huge capacity, but in order to recall this information, or even a tiny percentage of it, the memories need not only to be stored effectively, but acquired efficiently in the first place. It is these three stages – encoding (acquisition), consolidation (stabilization and enhancement of the memories ensuring effective storage) and recall – that form the process of storing and recalling any memory, whether that be a personal visual memory, an evocative sound or a fact learnt at school.

During the encoding phase, when a new memory trace is created in the brain, this memory is very vulnerable to forgetting, which is why the next step, consolidation, is important. It is here that the fragile memory trace is stabilized and consolidated in to pre-existing memory networks in the brain. Finally, if the first two stages were successful, the memory can then be accessed and recalled (although sometimes this is also difficult even though you know the memory has been stored – have you ever experienced a 'tip of the tongue' moment!), whether that be immediately, after a few days or after a few decades (2).

If we turn our attention to memory types, rather than memory stages, and think about the different ways we use memory in an average day, we can divide those memories up in to two distinct types known as declarative and non-declarative memories. Declarative memories, at their most basic level, are memories where we are able to 'declare' or express information, and non-declarative, yes you have guessed it, relates to memories that we cannot express; in fact, these memories are gained implicitly, and we may not even be aware, until we need to demonstrate the memory exists, that we have learnt anything in the first place. Declarative memory covers most of what most individuals would see as typical 'memory', and is divided in to two sub-types: episodic and semantic. Episodic memory refers to memory for episodes or periods of time, so this is the ability to recall memories or past experiences that are very personal to you – episodic memory can be likened to a diary, and within a typical working day episodic memories may include who you sat next to a meeting, how you felt during a presentation and the route you drove home that

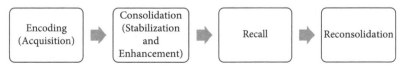

FIGURE 1.1 *The key stages of memory.*

evening. Episodic memories are often learnt very quickly, but are also vulnerable to fast forgetting, unless the event was particularly powerful and emotional. The other sub-type is semantic memory, which refers to facts and figures about the world. Episodic memory is different for each individual, even if they have experienced the same event, as it is personal to you, and relies on your drawing on your own past experiences and expectations, whereas semantic memory, which is often learnt more slowly, but is less susceptible to forgetting, allows you to have knowledge about the world, without having direct experience of it – an encyclopaedia, with typical semantic memories at work including the latest sales figures, the location of your new head office and the birthday of a member of your team.

Non-declarative memory relies on different areas of the brain to that of declarative memory, and relates to very different types of memory, those recalled not through descriptions or lists of facts and figures, but through action and behaviour (3). These include procedural memory for motor skills and perceptual skills, where learning is very slow (remember how long it took you to learn to drive?). A classic example of a non-declarative procedural memory is riding a bike, but more organizationally relevant examples (unless you are a bike courier) include the development of any new skill such as using a new piece of machinery, finding your way to a new office location or making a cup of coffee!

If we revert back to the different memory stages, two of these are known to be affected by poor sleep (or conversely, if you are a glass half full person, improved by good sleep), and relate to the question of when an individual sleeps, although the exact mechanisms by which this happens are still not fully understood. Going to sleep *before*

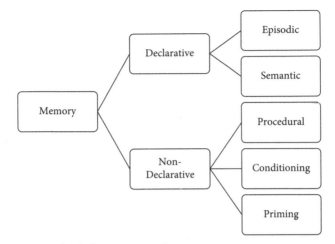

FIGURE 1.2 *The different types of memory.*

learning takes place (think of it as preparation), the pre-training phase, benefits the encoding phase of memory, whereas sleep *after* learning and before recall (think of this as percolation), the post-training phase, has been shown to improve memory consolidation.

There is now significant agreement amongst researchers that sleep in the pre-learning, or preparation phase helps the encoding of the information to be remembered, which then enhances recall of this information at a later stage. Such is the compelling research base that one researcher has concluded, based on their own neuroimaging studies of sleep deprived individuals, that poor sleep 'critically compromises the neural and behavioural capacity for committing new experiences to memory' (5), with sleep deprivation resulting in poorer performance in a variety of declarative memory experiments including semantic tasks such as verbal learning (6) and episodic memories such as memory for emotional material (7). Given that we could not possibly sleep before we try and learn every new piece of information, it is a relief, albeit perhaps not surprising, that sleep is not *necessary* for the successful encoding of new material to be remembered, but, the evidence certainly suggests that sleep can enhance the effectiveness of the encoding and thus the subsequent recall of the memory.

For the memory consolidation stage in the process, with sleep in the post-training phase (percolation), the story is a little more complex. Research on the effect of poor sleep on procedural memory has consistently shown a benefit of sleep, whereas the effect of sleep on declarative memory consolidation is less clear-cut. Added to the complexity is the pattern of changes in the sleep architecture found in the post-training sleep phase in some studies, and how this relates to memory and learning. Whilst science, like life, is never simple, there are, however, some key messages that can be drawn out of the growing body of research on the effect of sleep on memory consolidation.

Some researchers believe that aspects of the consolidation process can occur *only* after sleep, and some feel that sleep is a beneficial but *not* necessary process in the consolidation of memory traces in the brain, but most agree that there is a strong body of literature demonstrating the relationship between sleep and the consolidation of procedural memories (8), or memories with a significant procedural element such as learning a second language (2). In fact, the literature also suggests that it is not just sleep per se, but REM sleep, that is particularly important for the effective learning of procedural tasks. Researchers have found that the amount of REM sleep after learning procedural memory tasks predicted improvements in the task, with greater REM sleep relating to greater improvements (9), and that depriving individuals of the last two REM episodes in a night of post-learning sleep (yes, that means waking them up!) reduced performance on a memory task even when they were tested one week later! On the flip side, researchers found a 19–21 per cent enhancement in motor performance after only one night of sleep, either directly after training on the task or up to 12 hours post-training (3). For those of us who regularly need to learn new motor skills at work (most of us do develop new motor skills at work more frequently than we may think), whether that be grappling with a new procedure on the factory floor, being taught a new surgical procedure in the operating theatre or receiving a new piece of workplace technology, these findings are particularly compelling.

For declarative memory, that is our 'diary' or our 'encyclopaedia', the research on the relationship between sleep and memory consolidation has been less consistent, with some researchers such as Matthew Walker, at the University of California, Berkley, citing compelling evidence that sleep rich in SWS leads to enhanced performance on declarative memory tasks (3), whereas others believing that currently there is insufficient evidence to assume that sleep, whilst benefiting declarative memory in the consolidation phase, does so through any process that is unique to sleep itself. Instead, these researchers believe that sleep benefits the consolidation of memories relating to our 'diary' (episodic) and 'encyclopaedia' (semantic) memory only through the lack of interference and distraction when an individual is asleep (10).

Now, whilst it may be difficult to separate out the benefit to the consolidation of memory from passage of time per se, or the benefit of the lack of interference and distraction, versus the specific benefit of sleep (although some researchers have tried to do this), and thus categorically argue that it is something inherently unique to sleep, that is the critical factor, does it actually matter? From a purely pragmatic perspective, whether sleep is 'special' in how it improves memory consolidation performance, or whether sleep just gives us time free of distractions to consolidate memories more effectively, the fundamental message is the same – good sleep after encoding and prior to recall (perhaps with a focus on REM and SWS) can improve memory, whether that be memory for facts and figures, memory for events personal to you or memory for skills and tasks.

So perhaps we have come full circle – 150 years of memory research have shown that there is a strong positive relationship between sleep and memory, with memory performance improved after sleep. We can delve in to the memory and sleep literature to understand *how* sleep affects memory, and we can seek to understand if *all* memories are affected in the same way, and *which* aspects of sleep are necessary for improvement, but from a practical standpoint, the message is clear – good quality and quantity of sleep can enhance memory performance, and if memory not only enables you to perform your job more effectively, but also ensures you can find your way home from work in the evening, and shapes your very identity as a human, focusing on sleep improvements may be a worthwhile investment.

2

Can I sleep on it? – Sleep and decision-making

On 28 January 1986, the NASA space shuttle Challenger broke apart, approximately 73 seconds into flight, causing the death of all of its seven crew members, which included five NASA astronauts and two civilian payload specialists (1). In the same year, an official report by the Presidential Commission in the United States highlighted the decision-making errors made by key individuals, with these errors being made as a result of sleep loss and shift work in the early morning (2). The significant sleep loss experienced by senior leaders at the Marshall Space Flight Centre before the critical teleconference with Morton-Thiokol, the engineering company who built the shuttle solid rocket boosters, led the report to state that the decision to launch the shuttle 'should have been based on engineering judgements. However, other factors may have impeded or prevented effective communication and exchange of information' (3). In the teleconference, where these engineering judgements were required, Thiokol managers and NASA personnel discussed the previously reported effects of cold temperature on the O-rings (part of the solid rocket boosters), and yet, even with a severe frost expected the next morning, the decision was made not to delay the launch. This decision was made when certain key personnel had less than 2 hours' sleep the night before, and had been on shift since 1 am that day, leading the report to state that the effect on managers of irregular working hours and insufficient sleep (4) 'may have contributed significantly to the atmosphere of the teleconference at Marshall' and that 'working excessive hours, while admirable, raises serious questions when it jeopardizes job performance, particularly when critical management decisions are at stake' (3).

In 2001, Rolf Larsen from the Norwegian Military Academy conducted a piece of research on military students (cadets) who were on a training course. These individuals, as part of their training, had gone for four nights without sleep, and during the fifth night, again without sleep, they were put in to a situation where they were asked to complete a 'live' firearms training exercise, and were given ammunition and a firearm. Their task was to carry out an attack in the dark, with live ammunition, on a camp, which included a camp fire, tents and realistic dummy figures who were placed sitting and standing around the camp-site. In previous exercises, the cadets had been required to fire at similar dummies; however, unbeknown to them, in this exercise, the dummies were replaced with real humans, the 'live' ammunition was secretly replaced with blanks, and the firing mechanism of the guns removed.

Out of forty-four cadets on the training course, how many do you think fired their gun, believing the ammunition was live, and not knowing their gun had been tampered with to prevent firing? Twenty-six army cadets opened fire, with many firing several times, becoming increasingly frustrated by the guns 'malfunction' (not knowing the firing bolt had been removed). Fifteen of those that fired reported seeing nothing unusual in the target area, possibly due to poor attention and reduced visual acuity caused by acute sleep deprivation, but perhaps more surprising (or maybe not so surprising given what we now know about sleep deprivation and decision-making), eleven of the army cadets who pulled the trigger admitted that they had noticed 'movements' or 'living humans' in the firing areas, and six of them expressed doubts or insecurities about whether or not to fire. And yet, all eleven of these cadets followed orders and discharged their weapon. After five nights of total sleep deprivation, 59 per cent of the army trainees fired, what they believed to be live ammunition, at live human targets (5).

Within the field of business, few, if any of us, are responsible for decisions regarding the launch of astronauts into space, and I very much doubt that many of us are required to use firearms at work after five consecutive nights of total sleep deprivation, however, let's be very clear, many of us *are* making decisions that can affect the health and well-being of individuals every day, and may be doing so on poor quality or quantity of sleep, whether this be acute or chronic. For example, think about every time you make the decision to drive your car when you are tired. Research has found that single vehicle accidents, where falling asleep at the wheel has been given as the cause, are most common between midnight and 7 am, with a peak between 1 am and 4 am, the time corresponding to the greatest period of drowsiness (6 and 7). Think about working on the factory floor, operating a fork lift truck or even meeting with a direct report who wants to discuss a personal issue with you. Each of these scenarios requires you to make a decision or series of decisions, the consequences of which can affect the health and well-being of those around you. Just as importantly, it doesn't take five nights of sleep deprivation for these decisions to be affected. The Challenger space shuttle personnel were operating on reduced sleep, but certainly not at the level seen in military sleep deprivation studies. In fact, it can take just *one night* of no sleep before the decision-making is negatively impacted.

In 1995, a study was conducted with on-call anaesthetists, after just one night of sleep loss (these doctors reported to have had less than 30 minutes of sleep during their night shift). Following this night of very poor sleep, the anaesthetists were significantly less innovative in their thinking (8). That is, when they were required, in a spur-of-the-moment decision, to use a novel and flexible approach to solving a problem, their lack of sleep impaired their ability to be innovative in their decision-making. However, when sleep deprived doctors and medical students were given a routine or familiar task, which was comprehending detailed and lengthy medical journal articles (a task which may cause many of us to fall asleep!), they completed this without any reduction in performance, despite having to assimilate large volumes of complex information; the task was not sensitive to the one night of sleep loss (10). When an operation is going according to plan, then a doctor may not be required to be innovative. In fact, I expect this is actively discouraged. However, what happens when a medical procedure or diagnosis is not going to plan, and the usual tried and tested measures that a doctor would try fail? This is when innovation, flexible thinking and medical creativity may really be needed.

These findings start to highlight two important aspects of the literature on sleep and decision-making. Firstly, as Jim Horne, Emeritus Professor at Loughborough University Sleep Lab, emphasizes, it takes

Just one night of sleep loss to fundamentally affect specific types of decisions and particular cognitive processes that are used in real-world decision-making (9). One night of having no sleep because you were caring for a sick child, or one night of no sleep because you were up finishing a report, or on multiple teleconferences to your geographically dispersed team, can have a negative impact on the quality of the decisions you are making, regardless of your technical expertise, your skill set and training or your high-tech equipment. Secondly, there are specific aspects of the decision-making process and specific types of decisions that are particularly affected.

If we think about the type of decisions made every day in a business environment we can identify three main categories. The first covers decisions that are very routine: boring, monotonous, relatively automatic-type decisions that are highly learnt. Decisions that we make every day and perhaps don't even consider them as decisions because we do them so quickly, and in such an automatic way, without any real focused thought. The second group of decisions we make are during complex tasks, where we are gathering and processing large amounts of information, but the approach and the decision are relatively rule-based, and involve what is known as convergent thinking where we are drawing upon our previous experiences of what has worked in the past. IQ-type tests fall into this category, and other examples include writing a quarterly budget report or repairing a piece of faulty machinery. Finally, the third type of decision we make in a business environment are those that rely heavily or exclusively on divergent thinking. That is, decisions that need a high level of creativity, of innovation and of flexibility in thinking, where we haven't experienced the situation before and therefore can't draw on previous knowledge, or, perhaps, shouldn't draw on previous experiences because the situation is novel and requires a different approach. These types of decisions are extremely common during crises and unforeseen events (10) and are often high stakes (in terms of human well-being or in terms of financial consequences). It is worth emphasizing here that these types of decisions are likely to become more common as individuals become more senior in organizations. Senior leaders, working in an ever more VUCA world (volatile, uncertain, complex and ambiguous), are increasingly operating with little information, the accuracy of which may be difficult to determine, with no 'blueprint' of how to do things, and in a rapidly changing environment. In a recent piece of research, I conducted with a colleague at Ashridge Executive Education, we found that these very senior leaders, who may well be faced with the need for divergent thinking on a very regular basis, are those that self-report the least amount of sleep per night (11).

Each of these different types of decision-making is used every day in business, and each is affected in a slightly different way by poor sleep. The first category of decisions, those that are highly repetitive, relatively mundane and may be seen as quite boring, are *extremely sensitive* to sleep loss, for the very reason that they are boring and mundane. This is perhaps surprising given that we may feel that when we are tired it is this type of decision we can rely on because it doesn't take too much cognitive effort. However, when we become tired, and struggle to find motivation, these tasks that offer little excitement or engagement are often completed very poorly, usually much slower than usual, with multiple errors (12). If we compare this to the second type of decision we commonly use in organizational life, that of complex, but rule-based convergent thinking, these decisions are much more robust in the face of sleep deprivation. Robust, but not infallible, with research demonstrating that it takes up to 36 hours or more of sleep deprivation before noticeable deficits occur (13). What is interesting to point out here, though, is that if these complex, rule-based decisions are used very frequently by individuals, and so eventually become more mundane and highly learnt, then the decisions become part of the first category, and become more vulnerable to sleep loss again. For both of these types of tasks, however, a degree of sleep loss has been shown to be counteracted by the consumption of caffeine, and by financial incentives (14) or by completing the decision as part of a group (15), as both financial reward and social interaction can increase motivation and, therefore, engagement in the task.

The final category of decision, that with higher risk (and potentially higher reward), that may be more common (but certainly not exclusive) in senior leaders, is a complex process with many component parts. At each level of this complex process there is a danger that sleep deprivation (remember, just one night of no sleep) can reduce performance. These reductions in performance can occur even if you are motivated to perform, even if the whole decision-making process takes less than 10 minutes to complete, and despite the stakes potentially being high (14). Of course, describing the effects of poor decision-making in these circumstances as 'reduction in performance' may be appropriate for laboratory-based studies, but significantly underestimates the impact of such poor decisions in the real world. On 6 January 1986, console operators at the Kennedy Space Centre mistakenly drained 18,000 pounds of liquid oxygen from the Columbia space shuttle, just 5 minutes before launch. The launch was aborted only 31 seconds before lift-off, and only because the initial mistake led to a secondary issue that was detected. Console operators are highly intelligent, highly trained staff, working in a highly motivating environment, with high stakes. And yet, operator fatigue, as a result of being 11 hours into their third 12-hour night shift, was cited as 'one of the major factors contributing to this incident' (16). If non-NASA examples are needed, then both the 1979 Three Mile Island nuclear catastrophe (the most serious in the United States) and Chernobyl (the most serious in the world) are officially recognized as being caused by human error in decision-making and flawed corrective action, and both occurred during the early hours of the morning (4 am for Three Mile Island and 1.23 am for Chernobyl (2)).

This real-world, complex and dynamic decision-making, that requires divergent thinking, involves multiple component parts including:

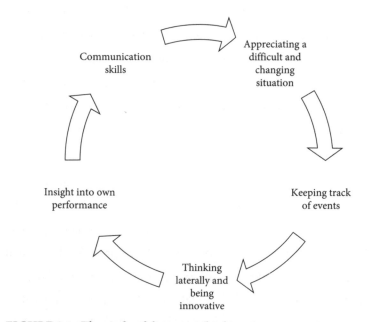

FIGURE 2.1 *The circle of divergent thinking.*

'The first step in the decision-making process is the ability to focus your attention on the task at hand, and avoid distractions. We know from the research on logical, convergent thinking–type tasks that assimilating or taking in all of the information is not going to be too difficult with one night of sleep deprivation, and, in fact, may still be possible with two nights of poor sleep. However, sleep deprivation of just one single night does mean that we may struggle to retain focused attention with it becoming much more difficult to avoid or ignore distractions, whether those distractions are visual or noise. Although there is little research examining why sleep has the effect of making individuals less able to ignore random distractions, both the neuropsychology and sleep literature does show a robust effect. In 2008, Mathias Basner and colleagues set out to demonstrate the impact of night shifts and lack of sleep on attention and vigilance, in a very real-world task – screening for weapons in airport luggage. The participants in this experiment (it was lab-based to ensure the study was robust, but designed to reflect the real-world security screening environment) were asked to screen individual X-rays of 200 bags in each test session, with 25 per cent of the bags concealing either a gun or a knife. Of these 25 per cent, some were considered easy and some difficult to spot (determined by the other random 'distractions' in the luggage and level of concealment). Basner found that the level of successful detection of the concealed weapon decreased and the number of false alarms increased both during a night shift, and after a night of sleep loss, with general performance being relatively constant until individuals had been awake for 16 hours (think of just a long day at work), after which detection performance deteriorated quickly, with the worst performance at 7 am after 23 hours awake. While the detection rate after sleep loss reduced by just under 4 per cent, and the individuals in this experiment were not trained professionals, the impact of this, scaled to take account of the number of bags screened in airport security around the world every year (700 million in the United States alone in 2008), is vast, and the consequences of a missed knife or gun, potentially catastrophic (17).

The second aspect of the divergent decision-making process is the need to keep track of events. If a decision is complex, then you will be gathering information, or information will be gathered for you, and when you have this data you will be making decisions about what to do next. Do you ignore it? Do you ask for more data? Do you act upon the information you have at that time? Are things changing? Is the data accurate? What sources has the information come from? Whatever the decision, you will need to consider the available information, and update your strategy based upon this. It is this strategic updating and keeping track of events that is also particularly vulnerable to sleep loss. In a situation where the rule-based decisions are not appropriate, where 1+1 may not equal 2, individuals who are tired often fail to update their strategic decisions based on the information, and instead rely on 'tried and tested' methods, failing to revise their original strategies despite new evidence that these solutions may no longer be appropriate. They use 'set fixedness', a psychological term which means that individuals persevere with a previous solution, even when it is clearly becoming unsuccessful (14).

Set fixedness relates strongly to a lack of innovative thought and cognitive flexibility, the next critical step in the process. If we can't rely on previous successful strategies, because the situation is novel and demands something new, then we need to adopt an alternative, more innovative approach. The failure here isn't about the comprehension of the new information (we know that rule-based complex tasks can be performance well with sleep loss), it is about letting go of an over-learnt and rule-based solution, and using innovation and lateral thinking to provide a more relevant solution. Of course, when we are making choices between strategies, we also need to assess risk and anticipate the consequences, a critical component of decision-making. We know from the literature that sleep deprived individuals become less concerned with the negative consequences of their decisions when faced with a high reward (18); they become less risk averse when dealing with high stakes – a potent combination.

But perhaps all is not lost – if we are in the midst of the perfect storm of sleep deprivation whist tired, and we are making what is turning out to be a series of very poor decisions, then, as highly self-aware individuals, we can reflect on this poor performance, understand where we have gone wrong and take corrective action (otherwise known as changing your mind!). No problem, right? Whilst the impact of a decision outside of a laboratory may not be known immediately, self-awareness, both of the decision at hand and of an understanding of the need for sleep, should reduce or remove the repetition of errors. However, research has found that individuals who are sleep deprived become more confident about ambiguous or vague decisions, and that even when 350 milligrams of caffeine (equivalent to approximately 3–4 cups, and shown in the sleep literature to have a positive effect on some performance) was consumed, the caffeine had only a small effect on improving the task and did nothing at all to improve an individual's ability to monitor their own performance (9). This lack of personal performance insight is an absolutely critical point for the business case of gaining more sleep. If highly trained, highly skilled individuals are making poor decisions, and having little insight to correct these, even when there is clear evidence that the decisions are failing, the ramifications, whether these be economic or human, are significant. In business, we rely, particularly at senior levels, not just on technical expertise, but on a high level of self-awareness and self-reflection, behaviours which may be particularly vulnerable.

Finally, after the decision or decisions have been made, they need to be communicated – to those that are required to act on the decision and those that may be affected by the consequences of the decision(s). Communication skills are also critical in the previous steps of the decision-making process; if communication skills are poor, then it is likely that the information you request may also be inaccurate or incorrect. Even as early as the 1950s, sleep studies found that high-level communication skills were vulnerable to sleep loss (19) and in 1994, a study by Kelly Neville and colleagues from the Federal Aviation Administration in the United States reported more communication errors with increased sleep restriction among American military crew who were taking part in the Desert Strom operation (20).

So why does this happen? Why is it that complex tasks that are rule-based and require things like IQ, logic and convergent thinking are relatively insensitive to poor sleep, but the type of decisions that are more common in the business environment, that requires divergent, flexible and fluid thinking, are really sensitive to lack of sleep? Unlike the rule-based decisions, those that require divergent thinking depend heavily on the prefrontal cortex of the brain, and this is the key. Tasks that rely on the pre-frontal cortex are especially vulnerable to the effects of poor sleep. The pre-frontal cortex, which is about 30 per cent of the total mass of the brain (14), is the hardest working area of the brain when an individual is awake, and sleep is thought to provide a fundamental form of recovery for this brain region. The pre-frontal cortex is critical for the performance of a range of tasks and behaviours known as 'executive functions'; those aspects of behaviour that become more frequently required in more senior positions within organizations. These behaviours include attention, language, high-level communication skills and memory, as well as divergent thinking and decision-making, and recent studies using functional magnetic resonance imagery brain scans (fMRI) have shown that reductions in executive functions with sleep loss relate to reduced neural activity in the prefrontal cortex (21). In addition, researchers have found that sleep deprived individuals show alterations within their brain circuitry during risky decision-making that may bias them towards focusing on expected gains at the same time as minimizing their focus on potential losses (21).

Libedinsky and colleagues, in 2011, after conducting a study on the effect of sleep loss on decision-making, concluded that 'even a single night of total sleep deprivation can have dramatic effects on economic decision-making' (23). Given the Challenger, Three Mile Island and Chernobyl disasters, and the Columbia near-disaster, the consequences are more far-reaching. However, even if we ground our conclusion in organizational life away from the world of nuclear reactors and astronauts, a summary of the impact of poor sleep on every aspect of the decision-making process made by Jim Horne provides a compelling reason to reflect on how your decisions may be affected. He notes that if you are involved in a decision-making process that involves divergent thinking, you are likely to be side-lined by irrelevant trivia, lose track of when and what was recently said, have difficulty in finding the most diplomatic words to express your point of view, become more distrustful and fail to detect subtle changes of facial expression and emotion in others, become more likely to misconstrue another persons perspective and less able to negotiate (10) – and don't forget that on top of all of this, your ability to reflect and have insight into your own behaviour may already be reduced because of your sleep deprivation!

3

Something I dreamt up – sleep and creativity

How is creativity defined? What does it mean to be creative? It is very easy to think of highly creative individuals, whether they be famous people or those we know personally, but to define creativity is actually quite difficult. Unless you *are* creative, in which case you are probably finding this all very easy! Equally, it may be difficult to see why creativity is important within a business environment if you are not working in a creative industry or a role that has creativity as a central aspect. Why do middle managers need to be creative? Why is it important that accountants, social workers or intelligence analysts protect their sleep so that their creativity does not suffer?

The link between creativity and sleep has been a topic of discussion for hundreds of years, with a vast amount of anecdotal evidence cited, particularly around the relationship between creativity and dreaming. For example, it is claimed that Robert Louis Stevenson created the plot of *The Strange Case of Dr Jekyll and Mr Hyde* during a dream and that Mary Shelley's *Frankenstein* was inspired by a dream at Lord Byron's villa. If we move from the creative industries, to science, the link between dreaming and sleep is still strong. The dreams of August Kekule led to the notion of a simple structure for Benzene, a chemical present in coal tar and petrol (1) those of Niels Bohr, which consisted of him sitting on the sun with the planets whizzing round him attached by tiny strings, led to the development of the model of the atom (2) and those of Dmitri Mendeleyev allowed him to create the periodic table of elements (1). Supposedly, Mendeleyev, after three nights of no sleep, fell asleep at his desk and experienced very vivid dreams, and during these dreams, the idea of the periodic table, a way of grouping the elements based on atomic weight which made sense to scientists and laypeople alike, came to him (3).

Within a business environment, creativity is expressed, not through the visual arts, or through poetry or composition of music, but through that 'eureka' moment (although often it isn't quite as dramatic as that). Insight, or the ability to take already existing pieces of information or data, and combine these in new and novel ways (to 'join the dots') that ultimately lead to a greater understanding of a problem, and potentially new ways of behaving (1) is fundamental to organizational effectivity. For example, strategic thinking relies critically on insight and the ability to see the big picture, but to be fair, so does any organizational role that requires individuals to generate ideas and solutions, whether that be in relation to people or processes. Insight, like dreaming, is an area where folklore offers advice; that 'sleeping on it' will deliver a solution. The implication is that if a person actively stops searching for a solution, and instead revisits the problem after a night of good quality and quantity of sleep, they will gain new insight, and, as is often the way with traditional tales, it does contain more than an element of truth.

In a laboratory-based experiment, Ullrich Wagner and colleagues in Germany in 2004 asked participants to solve a mathematical puzzle. Yes, the irony is not lost, that studies examining the relationship between sleep and creativity are often conducted in the laboratory. However, if there is one sure way to dramatically hinder the creative process in the real world it is to constantly follow somebody around with a notebook or computer, waiting for the creative process to 'emerge', hence the reliance on lab-based studies. Back to Wagner and his mathematical puzzles – participants were trained on one day, and tested the following day. Some individuals were asked to sleep between training and testing, while others were not. Remarkably, the study found that of those individuals who had the night's sleep, the next day nearly 60 per cent of them were able to see a hidden rule to solve the maths puzzle, whereas only 25 per cent of those who did not sleep gained the same level of insight. This rule was present during the training session, but participants didn't realize it, and yet nearly 60 per cent of those individuals who had 'slept on the problem' identified the shortcut solution, more than twice as many compared with those without sleep. This is despite none of the participants being aware there was a short cut to find in the first place! What is really important in this study is that this experiment was very cleverly designed, with a series of controls in place, so that the poorer performance could not be put down to fatigue, or that participants were working against their natural circadian rhythms, or in fact any proactive benefits of sleep on the subsequent puzzle completion. Insight, a creative approach to the problem, was as a direct result of sleep, or the processes occurring during sleep (4). So what does this mean in a business environment? If one night of good quality and quantity of sleep can more than double the number of people gaining insight in to a problem, then the importance is clear. Why have 25 per cent of the senior team thinking strategically, when just one night of sleep can increase that to 60 per cent of the team?

The physiological explanation as to why the period of sleep enables us to have insight, to take all of these apparently unconnected aspects of behaviour, or information, and see something that wasn't apparently obvious before, is related to the region of the brain called the hippocampus. The hippocampus temporarily holds memories before they are stored in different areas of the brain. Think of it a little like a memory library book shelf, holding all of the memories until it is decided by the librarian, where each memory should be 'shelved' within the brain. During sleep, the hippocampus 'plays back' these memories (the librarian flicks through the book to help with cataloguing), replaying all of the memory networks in the brain that were triggered during the day. As these memories are repeated, the neocortex in the brain (head librarian) 'listens' and starts to integrate this information in to pre-existing knowledge- the memories already in your head (other library books that are similar, usually related in terms of meaning). Sleep scientists now believe that it is this re-structuring of memory that sets the scene for insight, by taking pre-existing knowledge and changing it to incorporate the new learning (4). This process, in effect, throws all of the cards up in to the air and allows people to start to make these novel, insightful connections. If we stick with the library analogy for just one more time – it is the equivalent of throwing each page of each book up in the air together and seeing where they land, so that seemingly unconnected pages in different books may be linked together.

If it isn't really feasible to follow people around at work, scoring their efforts on creativity and insight, and then relating that to how much sleep they had the night before, then how is creativity measured in the lab to make sure that it is as close to real-world situations as possible? One of the key tests that many lab-based studies use to measure how creative a person can be has the catchy title of the Torrance Test of Creative Thinking (TTCT). This is a very clever battery of tests which looks at both visual and verbal creativity in a variety of ways. Four particular aspects of creativity are measured, and these are important components of the creative process, whatever problem is requiring the creative solution. The first aspect is *fluency*. That is, how many answers you can generate to a particular question, with more creative individuals coming up with a multitude of different solutions to the problem presented. Related to fluency is *flexibility*. It isn't just about coming up with the volume of solutions now, but how many different categories of solution are considered. In this way, fluency is about the quantity of answers, and flexibility is about the breadth of those answers. The third aspect is *originality*, and the fourth is *elaboration*. Originality is obviously critical for creativity, and elaboration relates to the building of one solution from the previous one. As more and more solutions are generated, do they become increasingly more detailed and elaborate, with each idea being derived from the previous one, or do the ideas remain disparate, and relatively basic? These four categories not only show how creativity can be defined, they also help to differentiate between creativity and insight, and memory and decision-making, although all are obviously inextricably linked, all rely heavily on the frontal cortex, and so all are significantly affected by poor sleep.

Experimental sleep studies have convincingly demonstrated the benefit of sleep on all four of the basic elements of visual and verbal creativity (fluency, flexibility, originality and elaboration). For example, in 2011, Valeria Drago and colleagues from Neurology and Psychology Departments in Italy and the United States used a short version of the TTCT to understand the relationship between sleep and creativity in healthy participants. Each individual was asked to attend a sleep laboratory for three consecutive nights. Sleep labs, whilst not scary places, are unfamiliar, and so the first night of a sleep study is usually not used to collect data. Instead, the participants can acclimatize to the surroundings, so that hopefully, on subsequent nights, their sleep pattern is as close to normal as possible in a non-home environment. After the night of adaptation, polysomnography recordings were taken on nights two and three, and the participants were also asked to complete the creativity test on either the morning of day 2 or the morning of day 3. For the verbal part of the TTCT, individuals were either asked 'Just suppose you could walk on air or fly without being in an airplane or similar vehicle. What problems might this create? List as many as you can' or they were asked, 'Just suppose a great fog were to fall over the earth and all we could see of people would be their feet. What would happen? How would this change life on earth? List as many ideas as you can.' To measure visual creativity, participants were first given a piece of paper with two incomplete drawings. They were then given 3 minutes to create meaningful drawings from the incomplete pictures, and to give their 'work of art' a title. In the second visual task the individuals were handed a sheet of paper with either nine isosceles triangles or nine pairs of straight lines printed on it, and they were asked to make as many pictures out of these lines or triangles as they could in 3 minutes, again giving each drawing a title (5).

For some of you, as you read the description of this study, you may well be filled with horror, reminding yourself never to take part in a creativity study, and resigning yourself to forever being a non-creative individual. For others, you are probably already on the internet searching for an opportunity to take part in a study like this, or perhaps you have grabbed a piece of paper and have started listing all of the problems in the world that can be created if we can only see each other's feet! Whether you are channelling your inner creativity or not at this moment (and that will partly be dictated by how much sleep you had last night!), it is important to emphasize here that whilst these questions may seem very distant from organizational life, the parallels are certainly there. Thinking about what could happen if we can walk on air is basically the same as asking what could happen if we launch this product. Or, what could happen if we close this department down, or if we hire this person, or if we cut our budget here to increase it here. Creative solutions are often a critical part of organizational life, even when the question is grounded in more mundane reality than walking on air.

Drago and colleagues found that fluency and flexibility related positively to Stage 1 NREM sleep. That means that the more light sleep (Stage 1) an individual gained overnight, the greater the volume of answers, and the greater number of categories used to generate these answers. In addition, the researchers also found a positive relationship between deep sleep (Stage 4) and originality, and a negative relationship between REM sleep and originality. Longer periods of time in deep sleep led to more original solution generation, whereas more time in REM dream sleep resulted in less original ideas (5).

These findings show clearly that not only is creativity affected by sleep, but different elements of the creative process are influenced by different stages in the sleep cycle. So, the quality of sleep is just as important as the quantity. Without light sleep you may struggle to generate more than one solution, or the solutions you do generate appear remarkably similar, whereas, if you don't obtain good quality deep sleep, then perhaps your solutions aren't particularly original, which rather defeats the object of creativity in the first place. Given the significance of deep sleep for a wide range of cognitive functions such as memory and learning, the relationship between deep slow wave sleep and creativity is perhaps not surprising. What is not certain is why Stage 1 light sleep should be so important for fluency and flexibility, although it has been suggested that the reduction in norepinephrine, which occurs during NREM sleep, may be partly responsible (5). Norepinephrine is one of the chemicals produced when individuals are in a stress-provoking situation, and is often referred to as noradrenalin. Researchers have argued that stress, triggering an increase in norepinephrine, causes high cortical arousal and vigilance, and this high arousal may reduce or suppress the ability to make more abstract associations between events or data. After all, if we are readying our body to be prepared for a perceived stressor (whether that be literal or psychological), then we need to focus our attention on concrete and tangible actions, rather than those perhaps more abstract concepts. Put another way, if I need to run away from a tiger, I would like my brain to give me some pretty solid information on how fast to run and where to run to. I am not sure it would be particularly helpful if I started to generate more esoteric solutions to my problem such as 'use a hover craft' or 'put on your cloak of invisibility'. Creative they may be, practical they are not. With a reduction in stress comes a decrease in cortical arousal, and, therefore, the ability to make unusual and unique associations (6). During NREM sleep there is a naturally occurring reduction in norepinephrine, and perhaps it is this that enhances certain aspects of the creative process (5).

The negative relationship between REM sleep and originality is also important to consider, especially if we refer back to the beginning of the chapter and think about the power of dreaming for Robert Louis Stevenson and Dmitri Mendeleyev. If REM sleep reduces originality, does this mean that the idea of Dr Jekyll and Mr Hyde or the periodic table was not original? Have we discovered nineteenth-century plagiarism? No, of course not, because what is critical here is that REM sleep is important in creativity, but it depends on the type of task as to whether it *enhances* creativity or *reduces* it. For Drago and colleagues, success in the creativity task required divergent thinking, that is, thinking of a variety of solutions, often in atypical ways (5). As we know from the chapter on decision-making, divergent thinking relies heavily on the frontal lobes of the brain, those areas that are very quickly affected by poor sleep. In contrast, convergent thinking in the decision-making literature was often immune to the effects of poor sleep for up to 36 hours of sleep deprivation, and possibly beyond. This distinction is also important for creativity, as tasks that ask participants to be as creative as possible, but only identify the single best answer they can, have been found to be improved by REM sleep (7).

For our nineteenth-century authors and scientists, REM sleep enhanced their creativity, possible because of the occurrence of 'binding errors'. When we are awake, the prefrontal cortex helps keep us focused on the task at hand, screening out seemingly irrelevant information; if you are the type of person that gets easily distracted, blame your prefrontal cortex for not working efficiently! When we are asleep, the prefrontal cortex stops acting as our 'thought police', and so information can be brought together (or bound) in unfamiliar ways, and previously discarded or irrelevant information can sneak in past our usually vigilant prefrontal cortex. Added to this is, cortisol is increased during REM sleep. Cortisol secretion, whether when we are awake or asleep, has the effect of 'fracturing' memories, breaking them in to smaller pieces. As sleep specialist Jessica Payne, Associate Professor of Psychology at the University of Notre Dame, explains, 'The brain dislikes fragmentation, so it weaves narratives, and that in turn gives rise to novel thinking' (8).

Up to this point we have assumed that quality and quantity of sleep are important for the creative process, but what about chronotype? The influence of chronotypes, that is whether you are a morning (lark) or evening (owl) person, is pertinent here, particularly when we think about the stereotypical creative person, working late into the night. Are more creative people naturally owls, who like to work late into the evening, and then sleep late in the day? There is little research that has examined this in detail, but the recent studies that have been conducted do suggest that there may be some truth in this stereotype. In a piece of research looking at both verbal and visual creativity in art and social science undergraduate students,

Neta Ram-Vlasov and colleagues in 2016 found that verbal creativity was associated with longer sleep duration, findings as expected from what we have already covered on the importance of sleep for creativity. However, they also found that higher verbal creativity was linked to later sleep timing. The students who demonstrated greater levels of verbal creativity slept longest, but also slept latest, they were typical 'owls'. This is supported by other research that has found typical 'owl' characteristics in those individuals with high levels of both verbal and visual creativity. Individuals with early sleep timing (larks) have shown to use less imagination and intuition, avoid symbolic and non-concrete content, display less novelty seeking and be less prepared for novel events than individuals with later sleep timing (owls) (10 and 11). Of course, what is worth emphasizing here is that this association is about time to bed. The research tells us that short sleepers tend to be less creative than long sleepers (so quantity and quality of sleep are important), and so 'owls' are more creative only if they are able to go to bed late *and* get up late; they are able to maintain a long sleep. The difficulties arise when people with natural 'owl' tendencies, absorbed in the creative process go to bed very late, but need to get up early the next morning for work commitments. In this scenario, they are likely to be less creative because of the impact of short sleep.

Perhaps the most interesting finding for Ram-Vlasov and colleagues, though, was that visual creativity was *enhanced* by *poor* sleep length. You read that correctly – students who demonstrated the higher levels of visual creativity were those that had the poorest sleep quality (9). Before you decide to deprive yourself of sleep in order to design the perfect company logo, or before you decide on the new paint colour for your lounge walls, it is worth considering why visual creativity may benefit from poor sleep. Sleep disturbances have been found to create and alter aspects of perception, such as optic nerve dysfunction caused by sleep disturbance in patients with a clinical diagnosis of sleep apnoea (who have very poor sleep quality) (12). Individuals, after significant sleep deprivation, or poor quality of sleep over a period of time, may be delusional, hallucinatory or in a state of altered perception before benefiting from higher levels of visual creativity. If you are a painter who never leaves your studio during this time, who never has to interact with another human, never has to drive their car or go to work, never has to go shopping, and has food delivered and cooked for them, then perhaps it is sustainable over a short intensive period of creativity. For us mere mortals, visual creativity at what cost?

Finally, all of the studies we have considered so far have suggested that what you need to do is examine a problem, go to bed for the right amount of time and get good quality sleep, while waiting for sleep to work its magic, whatever that might be in terms of reorganizing memory and learning. In the morning, you wake up and you have that eureka moment! There is, however, a recent study that has found that you don't need to wait for that process to passively occur while you are asleep; in fact, there is something you can do to actively trigger and encourage the creative process. Researchers from the Behavioural Science Institute in Nijmegen in the Netherlands and Harvard Business School in the United States wanted to examine the relationship between sleep and creativity to see if this creative process could be aided by a smell or odour. The researchers had three different groups of participants and all of them were given precisely the same task where they were asked to watch a 10-minute video about voluntary work, and given the question, 'How do you motivate people to do voluntary work?' This question may be one that some of you are currently grappling with, and it shows that creativity isn't just about writing poetry or painting landscapes, but is about thinking laterally and with originality around concrete business problems. All of the participants were told that after a night of sleep they would be asked to come up with as many creative solutions as they could the next morning, no later than 10 am. The participants slept at home, and so, at whatever time they awoke, they needed to log in to a computerized system and submit all of their solutions, before 10 am (the equivalent to having to come up with your business plan for the first meeting of the day).

When the individuals were watching the video and given the question, two of the three groups were exposed to a pleasant smell (and one group were given no smell at all). The participants in groups two and three were not told about the odour, but it was noticeable, and was a pleasant orange-vanilla smell. When participants went to bed that night, group one went to sleep normally (that was the group that were not exposed to the odour), and group two were given the same orange-vanilla smell in a diffuser to plug in throughout the night, approximately 3 meters from their pillow. The third group were also given a diffuser to use throughout the night, but the critical difference here was that for this group the odour was still pleasant, but different (fresh tonic) from the one they had been exposed to during the video and question (orange-vanilla).

The researchers found that individuals' average creativity score was higher for group two (same smell during task and sleep) than in either of the other two groups. Not only that, but when they were asked to choose what they thought was the most creative idea from all of their own solutions, the participants in group two (same odour at task and sleep) more frequently selected the idea that was the same as that decided by a panel of trained judges. That means that the creative process was enhanced by a pleasant odour, but not just any odour. The odour needed to be the *same* when the task was being given and during sleep, and by ensuring this, the researchers actively influenced and enhanced the creative process during sleep (13).

Do tired minds generate tired ideas? Hopefully, having read the evidence in this chapter, you will agree that the evidence suggests that yes, this is the case. Both quantity and quality of sleep are important for all aspects of the creative process, with the possible exception of visual creativity. Given that Einstein is alleged to have said that 'we cannot solve a problem by using the same kind of thinking we used when we created them', sleeping on a problem may just create the different thinking we need.

4

Sick and tired – sleep and physical health

Given that sleep is essential for survival (1), it is not a huge scientific leap to assume then that lack of sleep over a period of time, whether that be a reduction in the sleep you need, or poor quality of your sleep due to waking up multiple times in the night, will make you ill. We know that poor sleep often makes us *feel* ill (2), and if we need sleep to keep us alive, then poor sleep surely must take some physical toll on an individual. Of course physical resilience is not just about personal success at work; a resilient workforce has superior performance and productivity, better health and greater financial success (3).

For the connection between poor sleep and physical health, there is some good news and some bad news. Let's start with the bad news. Clinically high blood pressure (hypertension), diabetes, other metabolic disorders and some cancers have all been found, in very large studies, conducted over many years, to be linked to poor sleep. In fact, in a large number of these investigations, the researchers have been able to isolate poor sleep as a *cause* of these serious physical health conditions. There is, however, some good news. While the effects of poor sleep are almost immediate for all of the pre-frontal cortex heavy executive functions we have discussed in the previous chapters, such as memory, decision-making, mood and creativity, the majority of the physical illnesses related to quantity and/or quality of sleep take much longer to show themselves, often over many years. That is the good news, really good news. It means that making sleep-based changes now *can* make a difference to your long-term physical health.

In a strange way, it makes sense to start this chapter at the end – the actual end – death. Understanding the link between poor sleep and what is known as 'all-cause mortality', an umbrella term to cover death by all causes, illustrates the potential seriousness of the effect of poor sleep on physical health. In these studies, the researchers are not able to state that poor sleep has caused the subsequent death of the individuals, but what they are able to show is very strong relationships between poor sleep practices and mortality. For example, a piece of research in 2016 took data from over forty studies enrolling 2,200,425 participants, with 271,507 deaths. Using complex statistical analysis, the researchers reported that there was a strong association between poor sleep and all-cause mortality. The really interesting finding in this study is that poor sleep was found to be both *long* sleep duration (>8 hours) and *short* sleep duration (<7 hours). Yes, for the effects of poor sleep on physical health, we need to consider not just a reduction in the amount of sleep, but also the effects of gaining too much sleep (and you thought there was no such thing as too much sleep!). In the 2016 study, sleeping for more than 8 hours in any 24-hour period (so that could be one 8-hour chunk at night, or 6 hours at night and an 2-hour nap, etc.) increased the risk of mortality, with those sleeping for more than 10 hours in any 24-hour period of time at the highest risk. For the shorter sleepers, sleeping less than 7 hours at night did not relate to death, but if individuals slept for less than 7 hours split across 24 hours, perhaps as a short night of sleep (5 hours) and a 1-hour nap in the afternoon, then the risk of death did increase (4).

Sleeping for more than 7 hours at night, or in any 24-hour period, was related to an increased risk of death, and sleeping for less than 7 hours in any 24-hour period (but not at night) also led to an increased risk. This research, stark that it is, is supported by a variety of other studies in the area, all of which show that in this instance, long sleep duration may be a greater risk than shorter sleep duration (5 and 6). There are, however, a couple of very important points to emphasize here. In other areas of physical health, such as hypertension and cardiovascular disease, researchers have, in some cases, been closer to making claims of cause and effect. Due to the vast sample size in this study, collected from over forty different data sets, with different experimental designs, and different participants with a variety of other health issues, the scientists can only claim a relationship, or correlation between short and long sleep and subsequent death. This is a critical point, because a correlation does not imply causation. An example may help here – there is a very strong relationship, or correlation between ice cream sales and skirt length.[1] That is, as ice cream sales in the UK increase, skirt lengths of the UK population get shorter. I am not for one second suggesting that ice cream sales causes skirt lengths to get shorter, or indeed that shorter skirts increase ice cream sales; there is just a relationship between the two. There is a third factor, temperature, that accounts for both ice cream sales and skirt length. As the temperature rises, more people buy ice creams, and as the temperature rises, people wear shorter skirts. The relationship between ice cream sales and skirt length is caused by a third factor, temperature. If we go back to the 2016 study, it is important to consider a third factor, clinical depression, as a contributor to the relationship between poor sleep and mortality (particularly long sleep), as there is a large body of evidence showing that depressed individuals often have very irregular sleep patterns and/or duration. This is why questions about sleep patterns are common in a diagnostic interview for clinical depression. In addition, sleep disorders, age, sex and other health issues may be third factors to consider in this study.

A second important point to emphasize is that, as we discussed in the first chapter of this book, sleep is a hugely individual phenomenon. There is no such thing as the 'ideal' amount of sleep. What is ideal for one person may not be ideal for another, and so while we should be aiming for the 7- to 8-hour target, it can and does vary from individual to individual. You should not use this as an excuse for not getting enough sleep, but it does mean, for example, that if you do need slightly more than 8 hours of sleep per night, and you are otherwise healthy and happy, then you are probably getting the right amount of sleep that you need. This is critical to understand, because a chapter on the physical effects of poor sleep can be a terrifying read, and creating a readership of insomniacs, worrying about getting more sleep (or trying to get less sleep!), is categorically not the aim of the chapter. Yet, even if we put to one side the potential contribution of other factors, including depression and individual natural sleep variations, we shouldn't try and escape the seriousness of the message – the link between both short sleep and long sleep and subsequent death.

The research on all-cause mortality and both long and short sleep highlights not only the potential seriousness of the connection between the two, but also the importance of the 'right' amount of sleep, with both short and long sleep potentially leading to serious physical health issues (through mediating factors such as depression as a mental health issue). The significance of both long and short duration is also at the forefront of studies that have examined the effect of poor sleep on hypertension, clinically high blood pressure. Persistently high blood pressure, which as a general guide can be defined as a reading of 140/90 mm Hg or higher, has been shown to increase the risk of serious and life-threatening diseases such as heart disease, heart attacks, strokes, heart failure, peripheral arterial disease, aortic aneurisms, kidney disease and vascular dementia (7).

There are a number of ways that the link between hypertension and poor sleep practices can be explored. First, there are experimental studies, where healthy individuals are deprived of some or all of their sleep for a night or more, and their blood pressure is recorded, both prior to and after the sleep restriction or sleep fragmentation (multiple awakenings during the night). There are also much more long-term studies, where individuals are followed over long periods of time – 8 to 10 years is quite standard in this type of study – to see if there is any relationship between their sleep pattern and their blood pressure, particularly any development of hypertension. Finally, there are what are known as cross-sectional studies. Cross-sectional studies take a number of groups of people, such as those who may have good sleep, and those who may have poor sleep (long or short) to see if there are differences in blood pressure between the groups. Equally, researchers could take a group of people with hypertension and a group of people with normal blood pressure (and possibly a group with clinically low blood pressure) to see if these groups differ in terms of their sleep patterns.

In short, no matter which way you look at collecting the data, there is a strong and powerfully convincing case for poor sleep contributing to increases in high blood pressure in the immediate term (in experimental studies) and to hypertension in the medium to longer term (in cross-sectional and longitudinal studies). For example, in a summary of ten studies investigating sleep deprivation of the first half of the night, the second half of the night, the full-night or more than a full night (36 hours and 40 hours) in healthy individuals with blood pressure within the normal range, every study found an increase in blood pressure, regardless of how (and, to some extent, by how much) the quantity of their sleep was reduced. The effect was there whether there was an entire night of no sleep, or just a night of partial sleep, it was there for both elderly and young individuals, and it was there for both male and female participants (8).

Of course, one night of poor sleep may raise your blood pressure, but if you sleep well the next night, and the night after that, and the night after that (and repeat), your blood pressure is going to return to your usual level, with little or no long-term effect. Experimental studies, however, are a real indication of what can happen. If one night of interrupted sleep can increase blood pressure by as much as 7 mm Hg the next morning (9), then it isn't difficult to see the cumulative effect of this increase over time.

In a large cross-sectional piece of research, helpfully called the Sleep Heart Health Study, it was found that habitual short sleepers (those individuals who usually slept for less than 5 hours per night) and habitual long sleepers (more than 9 hours per night) were more likely to develop hypertension than those who slept for between 7 and 8 hours per night.

What is particularly critical in this study is that the researchers wanted to go beyond the correlation between sleep and blood pressure; they wanted to start to attribute a cause and effect relationship. By using a statistical procedure, they were able to show that this relationship between hypertension and long and short sleepers was still present, even after other factors known to contribute to high blood pressure were accounted for. These factors included age, biological sex, ethnicity, existing sleep conditions such as sleep apnoea, body mass index (BMI), caffeine and alcohol consumption, smoking, symptoms of depression, diabetes and cardiovascular disease. This is worth emphasizing – the higher

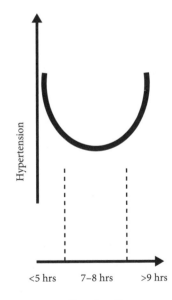

Sleep Length

FIGURE 4.1 *The 'U' shaped relationship between the risk of hypertension and sleep length.*

incidence of hypertension in the short sleep and long sleep group wasn't because these groups had higher BMIs, or because more of the people in those two groups smoked, or because long and short sleepers tend to have a higher rate of cardiovascular disease or were clinically depressed (which may have been the third factor in the all-cause mortality research). Even if all of these factors were accounted for, a strong relationship still existed between short sleep and hypertension, and between long sleep and hypertension (10). In longitudinal studies, those pieces of research where individuals are tracked for a significant length of time, the focus has been on the effect of short sleep, as long sleep appears to be less important in these studies. The National Health and Nutrition Examination Survey followed 4,810 adults for between 8 and 10 years, and found that those people sleeping less than 5 hours per night had an increased incidence of hypertension, and a summary of longitudinal research in this field concluded that habitual short sleep is associated with hypertension, especially during middle age (11).

While it is impossible to be 100 per cent confident that poor sleep causes hypertension, the evidence is pretty overwhelming that there is certainly a very strong relationship, and if a significant number of other possible factors known to cause hypertension have been taken out of the equation, what else remains? It is certainly argued by many sleep researchers that prolonged exposure to increased blood pressure, and all the physiological responses that exposure can trigger such as increased sympathetic nervous system activity (the flight, fight or freeze part of the nervous system), help to explain the incidence of hypertension in chronically sleep deprived individuals. Hypertension can lead to serious and life-threatening conditions.

You had a really late night last night, working late at the office and then again at home, trying to finish a report. You had to get up early for a meeting, and now it is lunchtime. You are tired, and a bit grumpy, despite your three cups of coffee this morning (and maybe a couple of biscuits too – just for energy of course!), and you are very, very hungry. You brought your usual salad with you from home, which is sitting in the fridge in your office. But somehow, today, it isn't going to hit the spot. Never mind, you will grab a take-away for lunch as you really need some carbs and some saturated fat, and will take the salad home and have it for dinner. You arrive home later that evening after another long day at work, and head to the kitchen. You are exhausted, you have worked hard all day, you deserve something more exciting than salad, so you ring for a pizza and put the salad in the fridge for lunch tomorrow. Sound familiar? You may not know it, but you have just experienced the battle of leptin versus ghrelin in your brain (in the hypothalamus if you want to be exact). A battle often won by ghrelin when you are tired.

Leptin and ghrelin are two hormones that, in combination, control appetite and the regulation of fat stores in the body. Leptin, an adipocyte hormone, regulates energy balance, and inhibits hunger when you are full – it is the 'satiety' hormone. In contrast, ghrelin, the 'hunger' hormone, signals hunger to the brain when the stomach is empty, increasing appetite. In a healthy individual, the two hormones, working in harmony, ensure a balanced intake of food (leptin helps to regulate the type of food we eat), and that we do not over-eat or starve. In tired individuals, this harmony becomes disrupted, with research finding that short sleep duration is associated with a decrease in leptin and an increase in ghrelin. The Wisconsin Sleep Cohort Study found that in over 1,000 participants, those who were reported sleeping for 5 hours or less per night had 15 per cent less leptin and 15 per cent more ghrelin than those sleeping for 8 hours, which could not be explained by BMI, age or biological sex, and was not a result of an underlying sleep disorder (12).

In a similar way to changes in blood pressure with poor sleep, the effects on leptin and ghrelin, over the course of one or two nights are mild, are usually very little to worry about, and will resolve rapidly when you recover your sleep. However, the size of these changes are similar to those seen in profiles that predict future cardio-vascular disease risk (12), meaning that while the hormonal variations may be small after just one or two nights of short sleep, sustained poor sleep can lead to more serious health consequences. A reliance on take-away food for a couple of nights, every few months, when you are exhausted, is not, in isolation, going to lead to longer-term issues, but chronic lack of sleep (in this instance, habitually less than 5 hours per night) may lead to fundamental changes in your hormonal balance, related to more serious physical concerns. This could be weight gain, as those individuals who took part in the Wisconsin study reporting to regularly sleep less than 7.7 hours per night had an increased BMI compared with those who slept for longer than 7.7 hours, but it may also relate to longer-term endocrine and metabolic conditions such as diabetes.

Type II, or adult onset, diabetes is the most common form of diabetes, accounting for between 85 and 95 per cent of all individuals with a diabetes diagnosis. It usually appears in people over the age of 40, but can be identified much earlier, and depending on severity, is treated with a healthy diet and exercise, or by also being prescribed medication and/or insulin (13). Given the link between only one or two nights of poor sleep and hormonal appetite regulation, it is perhaps not surprising that there is some very strong evidence linking poor sleep to Type II diabetes. For example, in a study conducted over a 15-year period, examining the relationship between self-reported sleep length and the incidence of Type II diabetes, it was found that both short and long sleepers were significantly more at risk of developing diabetes in adulthood. This U-shaped relationship, similar to that found in some of the hypertension and all-cause mortality studies, classified short sleep as less than 6 hours per night and long sleep as greater than 8 hours per night. Like the hypertension studies, this risk remained, even when factors known to relate to diabetes such as age, hypertension, smoking status, self-related health status and education were accounted for (14). Whilst explanations for the relationship between short sleep and Type II diabetes include weight gain and leptin as well as the effect of other hormones such as elevated cortisol levels (cortisol, the stress hormone, increases with a reduction in sleep quantity) in the evening which create insulin resistance (15), the biological mechanisms to explain the relationship between long sleep and diabetes are less well understood, although waist circumference (not necessarily weight) and sleep conditions such as sleep disordered breathing have been suggested (14).

In a press release on 5 December 2007, the International Agency for Research on Cancer, part of the World Health Organization, stated, 'After a thorough review and discussion on the published scientific evidence, an expert working group, convened by the International Agency for Research on Cancer Monographs Program has concluded that shift work that involves circadian disruption is probably carcinogenic to humans' (16). The World Health Organization has classified shift work which involves sleep disruption as carcinogenic: cancer causing. While I will discuss this in more detail in the chapter on shift work and jet lag, the point to emphasize here is the link between sleep disruption and cancer. The WHO has specifically noted that it isn't *all* shift work that causes cancer, just that which 'involves circadian disruption', and thus the critical link between shift work and cancer is poor sleep. However, while night-shift work has been associated with increased risks of multiple types of cancer, prompting the WHO statement (see the chapter on jet lag and shift work), the relationship between poor sleep and a variety of cancers in the non-shift working population is at best very unclear, and the majority of findings are often contradictory or inconclusive. This is partly due to the vast array of cancer types, and also to the multitude of factors that can predispose somebody to develop cancer as well as health and environmental considerations. There is a very strong and compelling relationship between poor sleep and some types of cancer, but this is predominantly in those individuals who have worked night shifts for a number of years, and so this will be discussed in the chapter on jet lag and shift work.

While not as serious in terms of personal impact, and risk to health, the common cold is said to cost the US economy more than between $25 and $40 billion per year financially, more than asthma, heart failure or emphysema (17). The effect of the common cold on organizational life is vast, and research showing the link between poor sleep and infection susceptibility also illustrates very clearly that it isn't just longer-term, chronic illnesses that can be linked to sleep patterns.

In 2009, Sheldon Cohen and his colleagues in the United States paid participants $800 to be exposed to the common cold virus. For two weeks before the participants came in to the laboratory, the researchers asked them to complete a number of questionnaires to understand their usual sleep habits. The questions looked at how long the individual slept for, how much time they spent in bed versus how much of that time was spent asleep (known as sleep efficiency[2]) and how generally well rested they felt. On the first day of 'quarantine' in the laboratory, the participants were clinically checked to ensure they showed no existing signs of infection, and they were then given nasal drops containing a high concentration of the common cold virus after which they were required to stay in the lab, under quarantine conditions (to make sure they did not contract a virus from another source) for a further 5 days. At the end of the 5 days it was found that those individuals who reported poor sleep efficiency and short sleep duration in the questionnaires they completed two weeks before being exposed to the cold virus were more likely to go on to develop a cold. How likely to develop a cold? Participants who reported to be sleeping less than 7 hours per night were nearly three times more likely to develop the infection, compared with those sleeping 8 or more hours per night. In terms of sleep efficiency, less than 92 per cent sleep efficiency meant you were 5.5 times more likely to develop the cold, but even a reduction in efficiency of between 2 and 8 per cent (so that is spending between 10 and 28 minutes trying to fall asleep for an 8-hour sleeper) leads to a 3.9 times greater risk. It doesn't stop there – these results remained, even when physical, personality and lifestyle factors such as BMI, ethnicity, income, education, biological sex, season of exposure to the cold, perceived stress, perceived social status, positive emotional style, extraversion, agreeableness, smoking, alcohol consumption and physical activity were all accounted for (18).

Small changes in sleep duration or sleep efficiency, over just a few nights, can lead to health-related changes such as increased blood pressure, appetite regulation imbalances and susceptibility to infection. Without changes to sleep patterns, chronic poor sleep can lead to hypertension, metabolism changes and Type II diabetes. Homer is said to have proclaimed that 'even where sleep is concerned, too much is a bad thing' and in relation to the link between physical health and sleep, the evidence suggests that this is an important consideration. Not only too little sleep, but also too much sleep, is linked not just to serious health conditions, but also to all-cause mortality. The business case doesn't get any more serious.

5

Got out of the Wrong Side of the Bed? – Sleep and Mood

In 2007, when President Bill Clinton was interviewed on the US TV programme *Daily Show*, he discussed his theory on how the relationship between sleep and mood shows up in US politics – 'You have no idea how many Republican and Democratic members of the House and Senate are chronically sleep deprived because of this system. I know this is an unusual theory but I do believe sleep deprivation has a lot to do with some of the edginess of Washington today' (1).

Edginess may be one mood characteristic that increases with poor sleep, but more broadly than this, negative mood is one of the most frequently cited effects of both short-term and chronic sleep problems. For example, in 2016, I conducted a piece of research with a colleague at Ashridge Executive Education, looking at the cognitive, physical and social and emotional consequences of poor sleep in a working population. Over 1,000 individuals of working age completed the survey, and from the sixty-eight behaviours listed, the most frequently reported effect was 'feel more irritable', with 84 per cent of the participants saying that this was like them when they had poor sleep. Seventy-five per cent reported 'feeling more stressed', 69 per cent felt like 'they wanted to be left alone', 62 per cent were 'less optimistic about their futures' and nearly half of the individuals reported that they were 'less mindful of their impact upon others' (2).

If poor sleep is so frequently reported as the cause of negative mood, and this is this supported by the research, which comes first, the poor sleep or the poor mood? Studies show, perhaps not surprisingly, that this relationship is bi-directional; that is, sleep influences mood but mood can also influence subsequent sleep. However, in a convincing piece of research examining participants' reported mood before they went to sleep and the following day, and comparing this to the amount of sleep each person experienced during the night, the researchers found that sleep the previous night impacted mood the following day far greater than mood impacted subsequent sleep (3). In fact, the effect of poor sleep on mood is so strong that in a review of the literature on the relationship between sleep, cognitive ability, motor skills and mood, while all were found to be affected by sleep deprivation, there was a disproportional large effect of poor sleep on moods and emotions (4).

The dramatic effect of poor sleep on mood and emotion[1] can be found in a whole variety of studies that span the sleep deprivation spectrum. An individual's mood is so sensitive to poor sleep that not only do studies with chronic poor sleepers and those with one night of sleep deprivation clearly illustrate how mood is influenced by sleep, there is also research demonstrating the effect after just one week of shorter sleep than normal, with the negative effects on mood becoming intensified as the sleep debt accumulates across successive nights of shorter than usual sleep (5). These studies also do not need laboratory conditions to demonstrate the effects; just a busy few weeks at work, impacting on how much sleep, or how many times you wake up, are enough to noticeably alter your subsequent moods. For example, Brent Scott and Timothy Judge, from the University of Florida, asked workers from a national insurance company to take part in a three-week-long study. For 15 days, participants were asked to complete a survey each day, with questions focusing on three aspects of behaviour. First, they were asked about their sleep the previous night, in particular whether they had any trouble falling asleep, staying asleep and waking up in the night. The employees were also asked to complete a questionnaire each day that examined four specific emotions thought to be especially critical to organizational interactions and job success – hostility, fatigue, joviality and attentiveness – and they were also asked each day about their current job satisfaction. Scott and Judge found that poor sleep the previous night contributed to negative emotions (hostility[2] and fatigue) *and* reduced positive emotions (joviality and attentiveness) at work the next day. They also found that that poor sleep in their participants was related to lower job satisfaction, which they put down to the increased negative and dampened down positive emotions at work (7).

This piece of research highlights some really important aspects of the sleep and mood literature for organizational success. First, it doesn't require any experimental manipulation of your sleep to affect your mood. Poorer sleepers are negatively affected in terms of their mood more than good sleepers, whether you are in the lab, in your own bed or working away from home. Secondly, poor sleep isn't only related to an increase in negative emotions or mood, but also to a reduction of positive affect – the double whammy. Finally, the link between mood or emotion and sleep isn't just about how you show up at work the next day, but can also be used to explain variations in an individual's job satisfaction. The relationship between poor sleep and mood, 'leaks', or perhaps gushes, into other personal and organizational domains such as job satisfaction, because mood and emotions are core not just to every interaction and every task we do at work, but to our very well-being. In a study looking at 'good' sleepers (those who had 6 hours per night or more) and 'bad' sleepers (less than 6 hours per night), it was found that not only did the 'bad' sleepers have significantly higher negative biases in how they viewed the world (such as a tendency to see negative events, expect negative outcomes and expect failure along with responding poorly to feedback and a sensitivity to negative mood), but they also had increased depression, anxiety and stress, plus decreased subjective well-being (8). Even if individual factors such as age, gender, household income, employment status and health are removed from the picture, well-being was *still* associated with fewer sleep problems (9). In fact, Nobel Laureate Daniel Kahneman found that not only is a good night's sleep critical in shaping well-being, but that the quality of that sleep was one of the most important predictors of life satisfaction (10).

While there is a huge literature on the effects of poor sleep on mood and emotions, some of the studies have looked at self-reported poor sleep, some have used sleep reduction (a bad night's sleep) and some have used sleep fragmentation (waking up in the night). While they all show, quite convincingly, that there is a relationship, what aspect of sleep is the most important? Is it all about how much sleep we get, or can the changes in mood occur if we just have a night where we wake up a few times, but still get our 8 hours of sleep? The research shows that quality of sleep is at least as important as quantity of sleep; on just *one* night, being woken up four times (10 minutes each time) in an 8-hour period in bed was found to be just as impactful on negative mood as restricting participants sleep to only 4 hours (11). While only getting 4 hours of sleep a night may be something relatively unusual for most of us, waking up a few times in the night (take your pick from small children, pets, noisy neighbours, full bladder) is likely to be a much more frequent occurrence, and this research found an effect after just one night of poor sleep quality. Interestingly, if the sleep disruptions continue over a slightly longer period of time (three nights), and become a little more severe (60 minutes of waking in 1 hour, and 20 minutes of wakening in every other hour for 8 hours – think sick child or very, very noisy neighbours), then while poor quality and quantity of sleep both increased negative mood in a similar way, the broken sleep reduced positive mood more significantly than the equivalent amount of sleep in one chunk. Having good quality of sleep, then, is as important as the right length of sleep, for reducing any negative moods, but is more important than quantity of sleep for increasing positive moods. We need to pay attention to the depth, not just the breadth.

Imagine you are about to give a presentation. It isn't your favourite pursuit, and you are not surprised to learn that fear of speaking in front of a group is supposed to be more common than fear of death. However, you have done a lot of preparation, you know your subject, and the audience should be friendly. You have practiced at home in front of the mirror (using your hairbrush as the microphone of course), and it was received with hugely positive cheers from your audience (your partner and kids). With your best suit on, you pick up your notes and step up to the platform. You open your mouth and nothing. You breathe, look down, start again, and nothing. Not only have you forgotten every second of your presentation, but you have forgotten your name, and why you are there. Your mind is a complete blank. Hopefully, if this has happened to you, the feeling lasted only a few seconds, and then your brain kick started, and everything went smoothly. The audience may not have even noticed, but it probably felt like a lifetime to you. In those few seconds, you experienced an amygdala hijack. It sounds very dramatic, but is very easy to explain. The amygdala is a small almond-shaped group of hugely interconnected cells, which sits just above the brain stem in the back of the head. Its role is to process emotions, particularly those that relate to human survival such as anger, pleasure and, thinking back to your presentation, fear. When the amygdala decides that there is a critical risk to survival, it can override the sensible, higher-level prefrontal cortex, and flood the body with hormones such as noradrenalin and cortisol, the stress hormone, preparing the body for fight, flight or, in this instance, freeze. While a presentation may not be literal life or death, it may feel so metaphorically to you, and the amygdala takes control, and hijacks your rational prefrontal cortex.

Why is the amygdala important in a chapter on sleep and mood? Research using fMRI brain scans of participants reacting to highly evocative visual images found that those who were sleep deprived showed more brain activity in the amygdala than the individuals who had a normal night's sleep, and they also had less activity of the prefrontal cortex (not a surprise given what we know about the vulnerability of the prefrontal cortex to sleep loss). In addition, for those individuals who had not slept, the path between the prefrontal cortex and the amygdala, which means we can effectively regulate emotion, was almost completely missing (12). In effect, the very tired participants were experiencing an amygdala hijack, the ineffective processing of emotional material because of the lack of 'supervision' from their logical and rational prefrontal cortex. The prefrontal cortex is also critical, not just for oversight of your own emotions, but in the ability to shift to somebody else's perspective, and show empathy with their emotional state. It will come as no surprise, then, that poor sleep can diminish your ability to 'read' the emotions of others (13) and show empathy towards others (14).

Try and think of one task that you do at work that is not potentially affected by your mood. Straight away you can cross out anything that involves any interacting with other people, so now you are limited to those aspects of your job you do in isolation. Emails, writing presentations, budgeting, spreadsheets, marking exam papers, strategic thinking, in fact anything that requires cognitive effort needs to come off your list as decision-making, leadership skills and creativity are just a few of the organizational skills affected by your emotional state and/or your general mood (15). It doesn't leave much does it? And, of course, negative mood isn't just about your own performance, as your mood, or the mood of others becomes contagious. Have you ever experienced that feeling of dread when you know you have a meeting with a particular individual? It isn't because they are unpleasant, or you dislike them. It isn't because they cannot do their job. It is because you know, no matter how happy or positive you are feeling before you enter their office, within a few minutes of being in their company you will be drained of every ounce of positive energy you had. They just have the ability to suck the energy out of the room, like the dementors in Harry Potter or Eeyore in Winnie the Pooh. Equally, there are people whom we work with that have the opposite effect. If you are having a really bad day, just grabbing a coffee with them will be enough to lift your spirits. They are the Tigger character in Winnie the Pooh, always happy and bouncing around. This sharing of emotion from person to person usually happens entirely without intention or awareness, and starts by the copying on non-verbal behaviours such as facial expressions and movements, until we feel their emotional state – emotional contagion (15).

Positive mood and emotions are so core to organizational success that a recent summary analysis of a range of studies examining the effect of these on work performance measures found that an individual's tendency to report positive moods and emotions was linked to:

- Superior negotiating ability,
- Better evaluations from line managers or supervisors,
- Discretionary effort at work and
- Higher income (16).

In the field of sales, positive mood towards customers has been found to predict sales performance (17), and, more generally, it relates to:

- Careful, systematic and thorough processing during decision-making (18);

- Greater decision-making accuracy (19);

- Increased creativity (20 and 21);

- Reduced absence and intention to leave an organization (22) and

- More effective conflict resolution (more likely to end in a 'win-win') (23).

More positive affect is significantly related to a wealth of organizational outcomes, both in terms of your own individual performance, and, through emotional contagion, across the wider team and work context. If sleep is so critical in influencing mood, then surely getting both the right amount of sleep and the right quality of sleep should be a personal and organizational priority.

PART TWO

The Causes of, and Tips, Tools and Techniques for Improving Poor Sleep

Basic sleep hygiene

Along with the topic-specific tips, tools and techniques contained within each chapter in Part Two, there are some basic sleep hygiene guidelines that will help you gain more restful sleep.

- Establish a regular bedtime routine
  - A regular routine allows the body to build in consistent patterns of sleep, and helps improve both the quantity and quality of sleep. Treat yourself like a small child – have a regular wind-down routine and try and go to bed at the same time and wake up at the same time in the week AND at weekends (give or take 20 minutes).

- Use the bedroom for sleep and sex only
  - It is important that the body, both physiologically and psychologically, recognizes the bedroom environment as a space for sleeping. Any cues that can be connected to wakefulness, such as working, watching TV or using technology, will not encourage 'winding down'.

- Try not to 'sleep binge'
  - It is important to get the right amount of sleep you need every night, and this also needs to be of the right quality. Sleep binging, where you reduce the amount of sleep you get during the week, but try and stay asleep longer at weekend to 'catch up', is, at best, not always effective, and at worst, counterproductive. Staying asleep for long periods at the weekend often involves larger periods of light sleep

rather than the critical deep (slow wave sleep) you may well have missed out on during the week. In addition, sleeping late at the weekend may reduce your drive for sleep the next night, compounding the problem the next day and creating a vicious circle.

- Think about the levels of darkness in the bedroom
  - The sleep cycle is strongly determined by light and dark, so a bedroom that is too light early in the morning can bring the body in to a state of light sleep and wakefulness. Consider blackout blinds (or an eye mask), but make sure you have a good alarm clock!

- Avoid napping too close to bedtime
  - Napping can have a very beneficial effect, but napping too close to bedtime can reduce the drive for sleep (the feeling of becoming more tired as the day progresses). This may mean you are not tired when you go to bed; thus you may struggle to fall asleep, reducing the amount of sleep you get that night (and potentially increasing the need for a nap the next day). Try not to take a nap after 5 pm if you are going to bed that night (so not on a night shift).

- Avoid heavy food close to bedtime
  - Heavy and/or spicy food can take a while to metabolize and may be the main focus of the body whilst you are trying to relax and fall asleep. Leaving a gap of at least 2–3 hours is recommended.

6

Environmental Factors – technology, temperature and noise

Technology

In 1879 Thomas Alva Edison invented the first commercially practical lightbulb, and within 20 years of its development in his laboratory, lightbulbs were being used in factories across the United States, allowing manufacturing to become a 24-hour economy, and from that, shift work was born. Not only did Edison make it possible to stay awake beyond daylight hours, he provided a series of inventions to keep us entertained in the evenings if we should dare to be tempted to go to sleep, including the phonograph and the motion picture camera (1).

Whilst it may be unfair to blame sleep deprivation in the twenty-first century on a series of inventions in the 1800s, the move to a 24-hour economy as a result of the availability of the lightbulb was certainly a critical step. Not only did artificial light allow people to be less restricted about working hours and about socializing, thus encouraging a reduction in the amount of time available to sleep, artificial light itself influences the timing of the circadian rhythms, thus producing disruptions to sleep patterns. This 'double whammy' of sleep disruption would have been unlikely to worry Edison, who allegedly slept for only 4 or 5 hours per night, and expected his workforce to do so too. In an 1889 *Scientific American* interview he claimed that his employees would fall asleep in corners, and that he employed watchers to find them and keep them awake (2). According to Alan Derickson, author of *Dangerously Sleepy: Overworked Americans and the Cult of Manly Wakefulness*, nobody did more than Edison to frame the issue of success as a simple choice between productive work and unproductive rest (3).

Light intensity (illumination) is measured in lux, with 1 lux equivalent to the light from a candle 10 feet away, or the illumination of a surface 1 metre away from the candle. Given that both of these are almost impossible to visualize, let's put this in to context. Moonlight gives off approximately 1 lux of illumination, whereas sunlight can vary between 32,000 lux and 100,000 lux. In terms of artificial light, a standard 100-watt domestic light bulb is 190 lux, the lighting in a standard office building may be between 300 and 400 lux and a warehouse or factory where detailed work is needed could be illuminated up to 500 lux (4). Knowing these levels is important because circadian rhythms can be reset after exposure to only 180 lux (1).

As we have discussed in other chapters in this book, light is one of the most important external zeitgebers (time-givers) for the human circadian clock. The endogenous (internal) circadian clock synchronizes a range of physiological and biochemical processes such as the sleep-wake cycle and the secretion of melatonin, and it maintains a 24-hour cycle (rather than the 'free running' 24.5-hour cycle), by alignment to external zeitgebers such as light. To ensure the best quality and quantity of sleep, the timing of sleep should be in alignment with that of the biological clock, and the use of *natural* daylight, helps to maintain this. Exposure to light outside of natural daylight (i.e. artificial light), particularly in the evening and early part of the night, even at low intensity (180 lux) can suppress the release of melatonin (the natural chemical that makes us sleepy), and shift the internal clock to a later time, the results of which mean that we find it difficult to fall asleep at night (5).

According to the National Sleep Foundation's 2011 'Sleep in America' poll, the most recent poll that focused specifically on technology use and sleep, nine out of ten Americans (aged between 13 and 64 years) use a device for at least an hour before bed (6). Not only can the use of technology in bed affect the secretion of melatonin (7) and push back our circadian rhythm (7), using technology in the evening and at night, whether that be the TV, a smartphone, a tablet or an e-reader, also increases our level of alertness. As you will see in' the chapter on psychological causes of poor sleep, a 'busy' mind is often a reason that people find it difficult to fall asleep, and engaging in activities such as answering emails, playing games online and surfing the internet can increase the level of cognitive arousal at just the point when both physiologically and psychologically you should be 'winding down'. To support this point, studies have found that the more 'active' the engagement with the technology (such as with smartphones or computers), the greater the difficulty in falling asleep, and the poorer the quality of that sleep (8). Added to the cognitive engagement created by the use of technology is the fact that light exposure itself in the biological evening and night also acutely increases alertness (9). For example, research has shown that not only did exposure to a bright screen for 1.5 hours in the evening or night time for only 5 days delay the body clock by 1.5 hours(!), but also that participants did better on mental performance tests after exposure to the bright screen, suggesting increased levels of alertness, which was supported by the participants' brainwave activity (8). Let's just emphasize that point – using a bright screen for only 1.5 hours a night during a working week led to a subsequent delay in circadian rhythms of 1.5 hours, and increased alertness, which in practical terms is also likely to further increase the time needed to fall asleep. For those of us struggling to find the time to spent at least 7 hours in bed, the consequences of a delay in falling asleep by at least an hour and a half is significant – a potential 7 hours' night of sleep could be reduced to 5.5 hours, just as a result of using technology for an hour and a half before bed.

Overall, the majority of studies examining the relationship between the use of technology in the hours before bedtime and subsequent sleep quantity and quality in adults have found consistent patterns, particularly with the more 'active' technology. The use of computers in bed for watching TV or movies has been related to the severity of insomnia symptoms, as has the use of mobile phones (10). In addition, extensive use of electronic media before bed has been correlated with increased levels of self-perceived insufficient sleep (11) and lower levels of 'morningness' – a measure that examines alertness in the morning) (10). The impact of technology use at night on work the following day is a reminder that poor sleep can and does affect performance at work. For example, smartphone use at night has been shown to reduce levels of engagement at work the next day, with energy depletion as a result of the poor sleep leading to the diminished work engagement (12).

Whilst active engagement with the technology may have the greatest impact, even relatively passive media, with relatively low light illumination (compared to, say, an office environment), such as e-readers, can still impact sleep. A team of researchers from Harvard University led by Anne-Marie Chang compared the effects of reading a 'light emitting' e-book with a paper book (remember those?) on a range of sleep measures including suppression of melatonin, objective and subjective measures of sleepiness at night and in the morning and full polysomnographic recordings of sleep. Light from e-books is short-wavelength enriched, with a peak of 452 nanometre in the blue light range, a critical point because, whilst illumination per se (lux) can affect the timing of circadian rhythms, the internal clock is particularly sensitive to short-wavelength blue light.

Chang and her colleagues found that compared with reading a printed book in a reflected light, reading an e-book decreased subjective sleepiness, suppressed the usual late evening rise of melatonin, lengthened sleep latency (time to fall asleep), delayed the endogenous pacemaker and impaired morning alertness (5). If there was ever a business case for reverting to printed books, this surely must be it (publishers take note) – using an e-book in the evening and at night can delay your feelings of sleepiness and reduce the physiological 'aids' to sleeping, making it more difficult for you to fall asleep, and therefore reduce your alertness the next day.

Tips, tools and techniques to try

- Remove technology from the bedroom

    Given that technology use in the evening or at night creates the perfect storm of effects on the time to fall asleep and the time 'available' for sleep (10) through:

    (a) The reduction of melatonin secretion and the delay in circadian rhythms creating a physiological delay in sleepiness

    (b) The direct displacement of sleep in favour of using media (13)

    (c) The potential physical discomfort from using technology in the bedroom such as muscular pain and headache (14)

    (d) The loss of the sleep-inducing effect of the bedroom due to the association with media use and 'work' (15)

    (e) The cognitive arousal associated with 'active' technology (16)

    ○ Try to turn off all media at least 1.5–2 hours before bed.

- Reduce the amount of light

    If a media amnesty before bed is not possible or practical, then

    ○ Try to use a printed book rather than an e-reader.

    ○ Try to use apps (e.g. F.lux) or system changes on computers and smartphones to reduce the amount of short-wave length blue light emitted.

- Reduce cognitive engagement

    ○ Try to reduce the amount of cognitively engaging media use before bed by reading a book, or watching TV that is not particulate-stimulating (an excuse to read the latest chick-lit or watch TV 'trash').

Temperature

Human beings are endotherms; that is, we are able to regulate our body temperature (homeostasis), and we do this with remarkable efficiency, usually keeping our internal core temperature maintained between a very small range of 36°C (96.8°F) and 38°C (100.4°F). If this falls below 35°C (95°F) we enter a mild hypothermic state, and if the drop continues to below 32°C (89.6°F), an individual will become so sleepy that they become unable to move, they slip into a coma, and, without treatment, will die (1).

It could be argued that sleepiness, as a symptom of hypothermia, is an evolutionary failure, as laying down and going to sleep is about the last thing an individual with hypothermia should be doing. The relationship between temperature and sleepiness is so strong, however, that it only takes a reduction of about 1°C from the normal core body temperature range before an individual will feel start to feel tired (1). This link between core body temperature and sleepiness and the sensitivity of the body to even small core temperature changes has led sleep scientists to note that an individual's thermal environment is a key determinant of sleep, either sleep-enhancing or sleep-reducing. (2).

Have you ever thought about why individuals in Victorian England wore hats in bed? Why did our Grannies buy us bed socks for Xmas[1] and why is there a huge industry in temperature-regulating technology in the bedroom such as electric blankets, and 'cooling gel' mattresses? Whilst Hippocrates noted the differing body temperature of his patients on sleeping and on waking, speculating that sleeping bodies felt cool to the touch because blood was flowing away from the skin, it wasn't until the 1970s that researchers started to systematically examine the causes of this rhythm in core body temperature (3).

When we are resting, or at least when we are not running around like crazy people trying to do 100 things at once, our body heat is produced mainly by the metabolic activity of our inner organs, particularly the brain, and those in our abdominal region such as the liver, kidneys and heart. In fact, about 70 per cent of our resting metabolic rate is produced by this group of organs, but they take up roughly only 10 per cent of our body mass (4). To regulate temperature (maintain our homeostasis of 36°C–38°C), the 10 per cent of our body mass producing all of this heat needs to be able to transfer this away from the core. Most of our skin is too flat for it to be efficient for transferring heat, but our extremities, such as fingers and toes, are perfect. These areas of our body, known as 'distal' skin regions, which also include the nose, lips and ears (5), are round in shape, which is the ideal profile for the transmission of heat, and so our core, producing the majority of the body heat, transfers this to our distal regions via our blood, with this blood flow regulated by our cardiovascular system (4). Our hands and feet are critical to the process of dissipating heat because they alone have a special thermoregulatory system built in, known as AVAs (arteriovenous anastomoses). Whilst the long name is not important, unless it is the winning question in a pub quiz, their function is critical, because blood flow, through these AVAs, is 10,000 times faster than blood flow through capillaries (which form temperature regulation of the rest of our 'shell' – that is the 'proximal' regions of forehead, abdomen, thighs and infraclavicular), and are therefore vital to protect the core, given their speed and efficiency in dissipation of heat.

So, whilst this may seem like a very complicated system, it is, a very efficient one, and under normal circumstances, our core happily plods along at around 37°C, using our hands and feet as a speedy way to transmit heat away from the inner organs allowing it to maintain homeostasis. If this steady state is what is happening 24 hours a day, then why did Hippocrates report that his patients had different temperatures when they were sleeping compared with when they awoke? The more observant amongst you might have noticed the sentence that said 'plods along at *around* 37°C', and this is because there are variations. In fact, like the sleep-wake cycle, core body temperature has an endogenous 24-hour rhythm, rising to its highest in the late afternoon, and reaching its lowest in the second half of the night. In comparison, distal regions show the opposite pattern, with hands and feet becoming their warmest when the core body temperature is at its lowest. This inverse pattern is presumed to be because the AVAs in the hands and feet are regulating the dispersion of heat from the core, and thus will be at their warmest when the core is at its coolest, and will be cool when heat dispersion is not needed (when the core is at its warmest[2]).

Whilst the changes in core temperature are only small, they share a critical relationship with the sleep-wake cycle, and given what was said earlier about the link between sleepiness and hypothermia, it will be of no great surprise to learn that sleep usually occurs when our core body temperature is falling at its most rapid (6), and wakefulness coincides with a rise in core temperature. Core temperature minimum is normally between 4 am and 6 am, which is when we are at our sleepiest, and sleep usually occurs about 5–6 hours before this minimum when it is falling dramatically. An individual is likely to wake up when their core temperature is rising, which is approximately 1–3 hours after the core body temperature minimum (7).

Within the sleep research communities, the relationship between sleep and thermoregulation initially led to a 'chicken and egg' type of debate – did onset of sleep lead to or cause a drop in core body temperature or did the drop in core temperature initiate sleep? Academically, this issue is of course important, but it is also of practical significance, particularly if we are looking at ways to help improve both the quality and quantity of sleep. If drops in core temperature cause (or at least lead to) sleepiness, then manipulation of temperature (core, distal or even ambient bedroom temperature) may be a perfect solution for poor sleep.

In recent years, researchers have found that it is the temperature changes in the body that lead to sleepiness and wakefulness rather than the other way around. However, there is one very important aspect to this – it isn't the decline in core body temperature that is vital, it is the *dilation of the distal skin* regions that create the sleepiness (the reduction in core temperature is a consequence of this, but it isn't key) and research from three clever sleep studies by Kurt Krauchi and colleagues from the Centre for Chronobiology in Basel, Switzerland, demonstrated this perfectly. In the first study, participants moved from a standing position to a lying position (8); in the second study, participants completed a sit to stand test (8); and in the final piece of research, individuals were asked to consume ice (9). In all three experiments, participants had their core body and distal temperatures measured. The results of the first experiment found that when participants moved from standing to lying down, their core body temperature decreased, and their foot skin temperature increased along with sleepiness, what we may expect from our experiences of going to sleep. In the study where participants had to move from a seated to a standing position, the opposite occurred, with distal temperature reducing, core temperature increasing and no reported sleepiness. So far, so good, we want to be sleepy when we lie down and we want to be awake when we stand up. It was the findings of the third experiment that allowed Krauchi and his fellow researchers to separate out the role of the core and the role of the distal regions. When participants ate ice, their core body temperature decreased very quickly, and not surprisingly when eating ice, so did their distal temperature, *but* not only did this not cause sleepiness, the participants actually felt more awake. In this study, their core temperature was dropping, but participants reported to be highly alert. This can only be because their hands and feet (distal regions) were also dropping in temperature rather than rising as in the first test. Across the three experiments, sleepiness occurred only when there was an increase in distal temperature, regardless of whether the core was decreasing at the time or not.

Sleep deprivation studies, where participants are prevented from sleeping, but are in an environment designed to maintain their core body temperature at a constant level, still show increased levels of sleepiness (8), and so we know that thermoregulation is not the only cause of sleepiness, but is a very important one. If we go back to the analogy of the ball (Process C) and conveyor belt (Process S), thermoregulation appears to be critical for Process C (possibly regulating the secretion of melatonin), but is separate from our drive for sleep (Process S) which increases in proportion to the length of time we are awake, regardless of other physiological fluctuations such as temperature.

From a sleep solution perspective, the importance of distal temperature in Process C is great news – the distal regions of the body are easy to reach (not like our inner organs) and we know they are very fast at heat regulation, so it's all to play for – bring on the bed socks[3]!

Tips, tools and techniques to try

*   Increasing distal body temperature
    Laying down, in the first of Krauchi's experiments, reduced core body temperature and increased distal temperature, possibly because relaxation can lead to increased peripheral blood flow (thus potentially increasing the temperature of hands and feet) (10). Interestingly, a number of other activities we perform as we are 'winding down' for sleep also produce vasodilation (and the temperature of our distal regions) such as a warm bath, hot drink and sexual activity. Similarly, foot warming, through wearing bed socks (either heated or non-heated), has been shown to reduce the amount of time it takes to fall asleep (11).
    *   Try engaging in bedtime wind-down activity that increases the temperature of your hands and feet, such as a warm bath, and wearing bed socks. Any activity which may also increase your core body temperature (such as a hot sauna) should be done at least 1.5 hours to 2 hours before bed, but activities such as wearing bed socks, that will selectively

increase your distal temperature alone, can be done just
before or just as you get in to bed (11).

- Heated blankets

  The use of a heated blanket has been shown to disrupt sleep,
  presumably because of core body temperature rises as the
  blanket continues to heat up overnight (12).

  - Try and use a timer on your electric blanket when trying
    to fall asleep, so that it helps to warm up your hands and
    feet, but doesn't affect your core temperature by staying on
    too long. A 30-minute time is a good place to start.

  - Try and set your electric blanket to come on at a low level
    early in the morning if you suffer from early morning
    wakefulness (13).

- Ambient temperature in the bedroom

  The relationship between the ambient temperature in
  the bedroom, the humidity level in the bedroom and the
  temperature between the bed covers and the person in
  bed (known as the bed climate) also plays a critical role in
  sleep quality and quantity. A bed climate temperature of
  between 32°C and 34°C, with a 40–60 per cent humidity
  level, is when good quality and quantity of sleep can be
  obtained (14).

  With ambient temperatures that are too high in the bedroom
  (through central heating or staying in a warm country
  without air conditioning for example), increased wakefulness
  and a reduction in deep sleep (slow wave sleep) often occur,

particularly in the first half of the night (2), and these sleep disruptions do not adapt even after 5 days of continuous daytime and night-time exposure to the heat (15). Humid heat further exacerbates this effect, increasing wakefulness and decreasing slow wave sleep in the first half of the night, and continuing to increase wakefulness in the second half of the night.

- ◦ Try to reduce the ambient temperature in the bedroom, through turning down or off the radiator and/or through the use of air conditioning. If you would prefer to use air conditioning for only a short time because of the potential negative effects of long-term air conditioning use (including your electricity bill), then have the air conditioning turned on for the first part of the night only, when slow wave sleep would ordinarily be affected (2).

- If the ambient temperature in the bedroom is too cold, then sleep also suffers, mainly in the second part of the night, with a particular reduction in REM sleep. However, cold ambient temperature *does not* affect sleep if the bed climate is appropriate. Research has found that ambient temperatures in the bedroom of between 3°C and 33°C do not change sleep quality or quantity as long as the bed climate temperatures are maintained at 32–34°C (16 and 17).

  - ◦ Try to maintain a 32–34°C bed climate, particularly if you prefer a cooler bedroom ambient temperature.

Noise

According to a 2014 study, as many as 104 million individuals in the United States live with annual noise levels of above 70 decibels, and as a result are at risk of cardiovascular disorders as well as noise-induced hearing loss (1). If this figure were to be extrapolated across the world, approximately one-third of the global population may be at risk of noise-related health problems (2). In the UK alone, about 10 per cent of the population is thought to live in areas where daytime sound levels exceed 65 decibels, and 67 per cent live in areas where the night-time recommended levels of 45 decibels are exceeded (3).

To put these sound levels in context (4):

Sound	dB Level
Breathing	10
Rustling leaves	20
Library	40
Bird call	44
Quiet suburb	50
Air conditioning unit at 100 feet, or background music	60
Vacuum cleaner	70
Food blender or dishwasher	80
Power mower	90
Jack hammer	100
Live rock music	110 (average human pain threshold)
Chain saw	120
Military jet take-off from aircraft carrier	130
Jet take-off at 25 m	150 (eardrum rupture)

Given that a short exposure to noise has been found to increase blood pressure and heart rate (5), it is of no surprise that prolonged exposure has been shown to lead to increased risks of hypertension (high blood pressure) and heart attacks (6). Whilst the exact relationship between exposure to noise and heart-related illness is still unclear, it is highly likely that somewhere in this relationship is the factor of poor sleep. The effect of environmental noise on sleep patterns may not explain all of the heart disease–related effects, but such is the importance of the relationship between sleep and noise that the World Health Organization (WHO), in 2011, claimed that sleep disturbances constitute the most serious consequence of environmental noise in Western European countries (2). Even if we just focus on road traffic noise, perhaps the most common but certainly not the only environmental noise we may be subjected to on a daily basis, the WHO estimates that 30 per cent of EU citizens are exposed to road traffic noise that is above that regarded as acceptable, and about 10 per cent of people reported severe disturbance because of road traffic noise during the evening and night time (7).

What is the difference between sound and noise? Is there a difference, and, if there is, why is it important? Surely if I am exposed to 100 dB of whatever you want to call it (loud is what I would call it), it is still going to affect my sleep patterns, and therefore, my subsequent health and well-being, and so why does it matter? The difference between sound and noise may just be semantics for some people, but when we are talking about the impact on sleep, the definitions do matter. Sound is produced by any mechanical movement creating a motion wave through the air and whilst every mechanical movement will create sound, the human auditory system can only hear a specific range.[1] Noise, however, is always sound, but not every sound is noise.

This is because noise is usually defined as *unwanted* sound or sounds; it is a nuisance or an annoyance (8). This means that sounds can have a physiological effect on a person; that is, you may have heart or blood pressure changes, even if the sounds are not unpleasant or unwanted, but only noise can have a psychological impact as well, because it is seen as 'annoying' (8). Interestingly, researchers have found that the negative effects of night-time traffic noise on objectively measured sleep quality happen regardless of whether an individual is disturbed by, or finds the sound annoying, but when participants self-rate their own sleep quality, the impact is determined by whether a person is annoyed by the sound (9). This is a point worth reiterating, as it is important when considering what we can do to improve sleep quality and quantity. Even if a person did not feel that the traffic sounds were at all annoying, the noise still disturbed their sleep quality (measured objectively by movements during sleep), whereas when a participant felt annoyed by the traffic noise, there was no disturbance in their objective sleep quality, they just *felt* that their sleep quality was poorer. Even if we feel that environmental sound is not disturbing our sleep, it may well still have a detrimental effect on our sleep quality, and when we feel that noise is really annoying and is definitely affecting our sleep, this may not actually be the case![2]

As you can start to see, the relationship between sleep and sound is complex. Not only do the effects of sound on sleep depend on whether an individual defines the sounds as unwanted (and so it would be classed as noise), but sensitivity is also dependent on factors such as type of noise (continuous, intermittent, etc.), intensity, frequency and interval (such as regularity and duration). However, there are some basic findings, which help to highlight the important role of environmental noise in disrupting the length of sleep, sleep stages and overall quality of sleep.

Research has shown that noises that reach 45 decibels (just a noisy bird call) or above can increase the time it takes to fall asleep by up to 20 minutes (11), therefore reducing the length of sleep we can get, and the same levels of sound disruption can also wake us up in the early morning (when sleep is lighter, and so we are more easily disturbed) and make it more difficult to fall back to sleep again (because our drive for sleep is much less than it was when we went to sleep at the beginning of the night) (8). Whilst a noisy bird may be enough to wake a person up in the early morning, the meaning of the sound is very important in relation to how easily we are disturbed by it. Actually whispering a person's name is much more likely to wake them up than a louder but relatively meaningless stimulus (12). Not only is this an amazing adaptation of the human body, allowing sounds that are potentially more critical for survival to disrupt us, it is also important when considering ways to improve sleep quality and quantity. When thinking about reducing the levels of ambient noise in the bedroom by using ear plugs, often individuals are put off using them because they are concerned that they will not be able to hear a crying baby, sick child, burglar, etc., whereas this research suggests that if the sounds are meaningful then you are likely to wake up anyway. Of course, why partners do not wake up with crying babies or sick children is another matter altogether.

Not only does difficulty falling asleep and maintaining sleep reduce the quantity of sleep we obtain during the night, but noise also has an effect on the quality of our sleep, through a reduction in both deep

(SWS) sleep and in REM sleep (8), and the after-effects of night-time noise exposure can still be seen the following day in both an increase in stress hormones such as noradrenalin, adrenalin and cortisol (13, 14, 15), and in poorer cognitive performance (16, 17).

Tips, tools and techniques to try

- Ear plugs
  The WHO recommends that the maximum noise level in the bedroom and night should be no greater than 45 decibels, and that the average recommended level across the night should not exceed 30 decibels (18). Given that there may be a physiological effect on your sleep and cardiovascular function even if you don't feel affected or 'annoyed' by ambient sound in the bedroom, try and reduce sound as far as possible.
    - Try ear plugs to reduce the ambient noise, and persevere if you find them uncomfortable. There are different types available including those made of sponge and wax which can easily be shaped to your ear, so try a few out so see what works best.

- Closing windows
  Research has found that the risk for hypertension increased in those individuals who slept with open windows during the night, but deceased for those who had either sound insulation installed, or whose bedroom was not facing a main road (19).
    - Try closing windows in the bedroom if you feel that the external environment is too noisy. It is worth keeping in mind, however, that closing windows may increase the

heat and humidity levels in the bedroom, so make sure this is addressed too (otherwise you may solve one issue and replace it with another one).

- Turn off radios and TV before falling asleep
  Researchers in Japan have shown that when participants are subjected to 'meaningful' noise such as a conversation, or karaoke, they reported greater difficulty falling asleep than with the equivalent level of air conditioning or road traffic noise (20).
  - If you use a radio or TV as ambient noise to help you relax in the bedroom, make sure that this is on a timer, which turns off before or just after you fall asleep.

7

Psychological factors

Sleep deprivation, caused by poor quality and/or quantity of sleep, may occur through life choices or through personal circumstances that we have less control over. You may be restricting how much opportunity you have for sleep because of extremely busy lives, because you have a family and children to care for, because you work very long hours or have a time-consuming commute. Perhaps you work shifts, or do a significant amount of international travel with your job; perhaps you are the carer for your elderly parents, or for a sick relative. Or it may be that you choose to sacrifice an hour of sleep a night so that you can use the time for the gym, or to spend time with your partner, or to catch up on chores, start the latest TV box set or read that book you have been desperately trying to finish. The important point here is that whether you have actively chosen to reduce the time you have for sleeping, or whether it has been 'chosen for you' through personal circumstances, you do not currently have the opportunity to sleep for longer. Hopefully, after reading this book, and being convinced of the business case for better quality and quantity of sleep, you will make a choice to change your sleep patterns, but at this point, you may be sleep deprived because you are using all of the time allocated for you to sleep, and it is not enough (or good enough quality). This is sleep deprivation and it is not insomnia. Let's say that again – sleep deprivation is not the same as insomnia.

Insomnia is a clinically diagnosed condition, defined in a number of ways by specific measures. The figures for the prevalence of insomnia vary, depending on the criteria used, ranging from about 30 per cent of the adult population who self-identify as insomniacs, to 16–21 per cent when three or more nights a week of insomnia symptoms are used as the criteria, to about 10 per cent when daytime repercussions of insomnia, such as anxiety and depression, are also included in the diagnosis (1). It can be characterized by an inability to turn off intrusive, emotionally laden thoughts and images at bedtime, it can be an ongoing difficulty of falling asleep, staying asleep and waking up too early, or it can be experiencing sleep that isn't restorative, despite adequate opportunities to gain the right amount of sleep and the right quality of sleep (2). That last sentence is the critical point – 'despite adequate opportunities to gain the right amount of sleep'. Those individuals who suffer from insomnia not only have every opportunity to sleep, they are often so desperate to create chances to improve their sleep that they will go to bed earlier and earlier, and stay in bed for longer, in an attempt to get the sleep that they feel that they need.

Sleep deprivation is characterized by a high drive for sleep – being tired and being able to fall asleep, even during the day, relatively quickly, given the chance.[1] This daytime sleepiness is a reliable indicator of insufficient sleep (quality and/or quantity) during the night. Insomnia, in comparison, is characterized by a low drive for sleep – insomniacs struggle to fall asleep or stay asleep even though they may complain of general fatigue. Interestingly, when insomnia patients are sleep deprived, either as part of an experimental study, due to life events, or as part of a treatment plan, this leads to sleep deprivation symptoms such as daytime sleepiness, but no corresponding increase in their insomnia symptoms (3).

In this chapter we are going to draw on the insomnia literature because insomnia is strongly characterized by intrusive thoughts and images at bedtime when trying to fall sleep, and, similarly, a 'busy mind', being unable to 'switch off' and waking up with 'my mind whirring' are very common reasons given as the causes of short or disrupted sleep in working populations. The distinction between insomnia and sleep deprivation, however, is important, because, whilst some of the features may be similar, for the sleep deprived, the racing mind and inability to switch off impact an already too constrained sleep schedule, and so these psychological traits are an additional complication rather than a primary cause. For the insomnia sufferer, these symptoms are a key aspect of their diagnosis. In a now-seminal study on insomnia conducted in the 1980s, researchers found that cognitive arousal (a scientific term for a 'busy mind'!) and intrusive thoughts and images at bedtime were ten times more likely to be reported as the cause of an individual's insomnia than general sleep hygiene issues (4). Nonetheless, understanding the research on intrusive thoughts and patterns of worry in the insomnia literature has some direct benefit to those of you who are sleep deprived and who find their already too restricted sleep schedule is further impacted because you find it difficult to fall asleep or you wake up multiple times in the night.

Would you like to try a little experiment? Okay, find a quiet room (I appreciate that may be the hard part!), or at least a relatively quiet corner of a room and grab your watch or phone so that you have a timer. Now, read the following paragraph, and then follow the instructions underneath the paragraph:

'Whatever you do, do not think about pink elephants. No, don't do it, think about something else, anything else, but whatever happens, do not imagine a huge pink elephant with huge pink ears and huge pink legs and a huge pink trunk. Try and get your mind to go blank because what you do not want to happen is for you to picture a bright pink, ginormous elephant, no stop it, don't think about it.'

Now time yourself on how long you can manage to go without thinking of a pink elephant.

I don't expect you got past 5 seconds, or 10 seconds if you went into some kind of zen-like trance. The point here is that the minute you try *not* to think about something, that is the only thing you *can* think about. Now imagine you are really tired, you have had a hard day at work, and perhaps a few nights of very poor sleep. Tonight you have the opportunity to go to bed early, so you take advantage of this, and go to bed at 9 pm. You are lying down in bed, trying very hard not to think about anything. Of course, the first thing that comes into your mind is, 'I really must get some sleep … I've had a couple of nights of really bad sleep, I am exhausted, and I have a really important meeting tomorrow. I must get some sleep', and once these thoughts enter your head you mind becomes very active, the effects of the great wind-down routine that you practiced before bed disappears, and all you can think about is the need to get to sleep. Ironically, thinking about the need to get to sleep is one certain way not to be able to fall asleep.

Research with insomnia patients, who often spend a great deal of time in bed worrying about not being able to get to sleep, has found that attempts to stop or suppress these types of intrusive thought are counter-productive, and actually may perpetuate the issue. A piece of research conducted by Alison Harvey from Oxford University, in 2003, found that not only did insomniacs feel less in control of their pre-sleep thinking (described as pre-sleep cognitive activity) and were more likely to consciously attempt to control and suppress these thoughts than good sleepers, but when participants in the study were explicitly instructed to try and suppress a particular intrusive thought at bedtime, they reported it took them longer to fall asleep and that their sleep quality was poorer than those who were not instructed to control these thoughts (5). Trying to stop thinking about going to sleep will just make you concentrate more on these thoughts in the same way as the experiment on the pink elephant showed that not thinking about a pink elephant is a guaranteed way to make sure that is all you think about. Much of the treatment for insomnia, which is also very helpful for those of us who are sleep deprived and needing to quieten our busy minds, promotes the use of distraction techniques. Such techniques seem to facilitate the onset of sleep and reduce the discomfort associated with intrusive or worrying thoughts, rather than actually trying to stop or modify them (6) – methods of distraction and mindfulness are discussed in the section on Tips, tools and techniques to try.

The types of intrusive thoughts that you might be struggling with when you are trying to fall asleep have been categorized into six different groups (7):

- Trivial topics

- Thoughts about sleep

- Family and long-term concerns

- Positive concerns and plans

- Preoccupation with bodily sensations

- Work and recent concerns

and worrying or rumination during the pre-sleep phase can be categorized into eight different types, covering active problem solving, monitoring your present state and reacting to your environment (8):

- Rehearsal/planning/problem solving ('What do I need to get done at work tomorrow?')

- Sleep and its consequences ('If I don't get to sleep right now I am going to feel terrible tomorrow')

- Reflection on quality of thoughts ('Why didn't I come up with that great idea in the meeting?')

- Arousal status ('Why aren't I sleepy?')

- External noise ('Did I hear a noise downstairs?')

- Autonomic experiences ('Why is my heart racing?')

- Procedural factors ('I must remember to book a dentist appointment')

• Rising from bed ('I have an early start, I must not oversleep again')

Tips, tools and techniques to try

• Reducing selective attention

When we are anxious, we narrow our attention to focus on the potential threat in the environment, ignoring other, irrelevant stimuli. Whilst this is an extremely effective mechanism if we are faced with a genuine threat, becoming anxious and encouraging our brain to focus attention on the thoughts in our head when we are trying to get to sleep is not particularly useful (for solving the worry or getting to sleep).

In 2007, sleep researchers conducted a study to effectively demonstrate the disruption caused to sleep as a result of this selective attention. Insomnia patients were allocated to one of two groups. The first group were given a digital clock for the bedroom, and the second group were given an identical clock, but with one critical difference – the digits it displayed were entirely random (so it was useless at telling the time). The study found that not only did those participants given the 'real' clock overestimate the amount of time it took them to fall asleep, they overestimated significantly more than the other group of insomnia patients with the random digital clock. Perhaps more importantly, not only did it feel as though they were awake for longer, analysis of the sleep data found that in the first 60 minutes after the 'real' clock group fell asleep, they woke up more than the group with the random digital display – a difference in the quality of their sleep. Both groups had insomnia, but those that were able to focus their attention on the actual passage of time by looking at a real clock, and therefore started to develop anxiety around the need to fall asleep quickly, had reduced the quality of their sleep (9).

- ○ Try and reduce the anxiety-provoking stimuli in your bedroom by removing your mobile phone, laptop and tablet, and by turning your clock around (so that the alarm still works but you can't see the time).

- • Distraction techniques through mindfulness
  Interventions to improve sleep through mindfulness are based on the research discussed previously on selective attention. Rather than concentrating on the intrusive thoughts and feelings, or trying to stop concentrating on them, the practice of mindfulness provides intentional awareness of the present moment, including all bodily sensations, helping to reduce the focus of attention on cognitive processing. Studies have found a positive relationship between the practice of mindfulness techniques and feeling refreshed after sleep (10) as well as an improvement in sleep quality amongst breast and prostate cancer patients who practiced mindfulness techniques (11). For insomnia, the effects of mindfulness have also been very positive, with research finding a 50 per cent reduction in total wake time after mindfulness practice combined with

behaviour therapy, and all but two of the patients no longer
had clinically significant insomnia at the end of the study,
improvements that were sustained 12 months later for 61
per cent of the patients (12). Finally, a 2011 study found
that participants who practiced mindfulness had significant
improvements to their total sleep duration, and their sleep
efficiency as well as falling asleep faster – both their sleep
quantity and their sleep quality improved (13).

○   There is now a vast selection of books and apps for
    mindfulness available on the market, and which works
    best for you is personal choice. The main point is to
    persevere, and try and practice for at least 10 minutes per
    day.

• Creating a visual image
  Researchers have found that thinking in the form of pictures
  and images resulted in the resolution of the worry whereas
  thinking in the form of verbal phrases and sentences lead to
  the ongoing maintenance of that worry (14).

○   If you find that you are lying in bed worrying or
    ruminating, then try and convert your thinking into
    images, and picture the worry rather than articulating it in
    your head through words and sentences.

• Free-form writing
  One of the reasons why individuals often report a 'busy mind'
  stopping them falling asleep is the feeling that they have
  to remember everything they are thinking about until it is
  actioned or at least written down, and of course, when you

are lying in bed, the temptation is to keep processing all of the information, or try and force yourself to 'switch off' by telling yourself to stop thinking (which we now know won't work, it is likely to make you focus even more on the thoughts). Free-from writing is often used by writers to free up creativity, but in this context it is often a helpful way of quieting a busy mind by the 'trick' of feeling that everything that is being held in your brain is now out on paper. The key, however, is to make sure you leave at least 2 hours between completing the free-form writing and going to bed, any closer and the technique may just reinforce your thought processes rather than allow you the space to 'empty your head'.

○   The technique involves continuous writing, for a predetermined period of time (start with 5 minutes and then build over time to 10 minutes). Write whatever comes in to your head, without any concern about spelling or grammar and make no corrections (and what you write doesn't need to make any sense at all). Do not stop, and do not overthink what you are writing. You are not completing a to-do list, or a novel; you are using the exercise as a way of 'emptying your head' of all of the thoughts that are crowding in on you, but you do not need to make sense of any of them. If you reach a point where you can't think of anything to write, then *write* that you can't think of anything to write, until you find another line of thought. Try and write freely, letting thoughts lead where they may.

- Creating worry space

  Rumination is a fact of life – how much we ruminate will vary from person to person, but all of us reflect on our successes and failures, albeit more often the failures are those that concern us most. Trying to stop worry and rumination entirely is neither practical nor achievable, and in fact, recent research has found that some rumination can actually aid problem solving performance if the rumination is focused on actions (i.e. how to do something differently next time) rather than on how the failure has made you feel (15). However, when we ruminate is fundamental. If you have a crazy schedule, are busy for most of the day and your only really quiet time is in bed, then this is when you are going to take the opportunity to ruminate or worry, and this is when it is the least effective and is going to disrupt your sleep pattern.

  ○ Try to create a space in the day as 'worry time', and this should not be just before you go to bed, or whilst you are trying to fall asleep. Try and find a 30-minute period when you can find somewhere quiet, and spend that time in cogitation and rumination, knowing it is a discrete period of time, and that it is far enough away from your bedtime that it will not interfere with your sleep schedule.

8

Physiological factors – caffeine, alcohol and exercise

Caffeine

Caffeine is only one of two drugs that are both naturally occurring and added to a wide variety of foods and drinks (for the geeks among us, the other one is quinine). In North America and the UK, between 82 per cent and 95 per cent of adults regularly consume caffeine (1), with caffeine coming in various forms including coffee, tea, fizzy and energy drinks, chocolate, pain killers, cold and allergy medication, diet pills and even ice cream. Yes, even coffee-flavoured ice cream can contain as much caffeine as a can of cola.

According to a 2008 Food and Drug Administration report, the average amount of caffeine consumed per day in the United States is approximately 300 milligram (4–5 cups of coffee) (3), with the majority of that taken as coffee. Over 2 billion cups of coffee are

Product	Serving size	Average caffeine (mg)
Espresso	2 oz	100
Instant coffee	8 oz	40–108
Decaffeinated coffee	8 oz	5–6
Leaf Tea	7 oz	50–60
Coca-Cola	12 oz	45
Dr Pepper	12 oz	41
Red Bull	8.3 oz	67
Chocolate bar	28 g	15

This is US data – there is significant variation in caffeine (and sugar) levels from country to country (2).

consumed each and every day (it takes 42 beans to make an espresso), and coffee is the second-largest export, measured in US dollars, after oil (4).

Caffeine, consumed through either eating or drinking, takes between 30 and 75 minutes to reach what is known as peak plasma levels; that is, it takes only half an hour to an hour or so before caffeine reaches its greatest effect, but it can stay in the body significantly longer, with a half-life (the time taken for the amount of caffeine in the body to reduce by half) of between 3 and 7 hours depending on individual tolerance (2).

While you would need to drink about 75 cups of coffee in a relatively short period of time (4–5 hours) for it to be fatal (5), there is little doubt among sleep researchers that only a very small amount of caffeine can reduce both the quantity and the quality of your sleep. But, of course, the relationship between sleep and caffeine is bi-directional – yes, caffeine consumption, particularly close to bedtime, can lead to disturbed sleep, but poor sleep itself often leads to an increase in caffeine consumption the next day because of its performance and wakefulness-enhancing properties (2). This bi-directional relationship can, however, very easily become cyclical, with individuals using caffeine to stay awake and maintain a certain performance level during the day, leading to large amounts of caffeine in the body, resulting in disrupted sleep that night, creating tiredness and fatigue the next day. This is exactly what sleep researchers have found. Caffeine use has been shown to be associated with daytime sleepiness, with individuals who report the most severe sleep symptoms (a month or more of disturbed sleep) also reporting the highest caffeine consumption (over seven cups of coffee per day) (2), and the prevalence of sleepiness was found to be twice as high in high caffeine users compared to moderate caffeine users (6).

In a neuroimaging study in 2008, researchers, scanning the brains of participants, found that only 100 milligram of caffeine taken during a memory task (the smallest amount found to have any cognitive benefit (7) and equivalent to one or two cups of coffee) led to increased activity in the prefrontal cortex of the brain (8). We know from the chapters on the effects of poor sleep that the prefrontal cortex is a critical brain structure for 'executive functions' such as memory, decision-making, information processing and learning, and

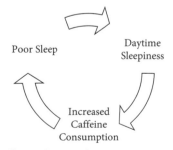

Poor Sleep   Daytime Sleepiness

Increased Caffeine Consumption

FIGURE 8.1 *The caffeine/sleep cycle.*

therefore it is perhaps not surprising that caffeine, known to enhance performance on tasks such as memory and speed of processing information, has an effect on this particular region of the brain, although doses higher than 200 milligram are usually required to see performance improvements in reaction time, attention and memory. In addition, the poorer the sleep of the individual, the greater the dose of caffeine needed to see the cognitive benefits (5).

Caffeine has also been found to improve both physical performance and endurance, and while these increases are not profound by any means, in professional sport, where any legitimate form of incremental gains are critical, and only tiny margins are the difference between success and failure, caffeine is often used. Such is the widespread use of caffeine in sport that whilst it was once banned by the International Anti-Doping Agency, it was removed from their list because of such prolific use across the world (5). In a study looking at the effects of sleep deprivation and caffeine on rugby passing skills in elite professional rugby players it was found that whilst sleeping for 3–5 hours the previous night reduced the athletes' ability to perform the repeat ball-passing manoeuvre, a single dose of 1 mg/kg caffeine counteracted the effect of the poor sleep to the extent that their performance was equivalent to the non-sleep-deprived group. In addition, the researchers found no difference between a 1 mg/kg or a 5 mg/kg dose even though the players reported feeling slightly nauseous and 'jittery' after the 5 mg/kg dose (so the larger dose was having a physiological effect, but not an effect on performance over and above the smaller 1 mg/kg caffeine dose) (9).

Along with the performance-enhancing properties of caffeine comes the potential disruption to sleep, both quality and quantity, even in elite sport. In 2014, University of Sydney researchers from the Faculty of Health Sciences conducted an experiment on male cyclists/triathletes who were asked to take part in an 80-minute afternoon training session followed by a cycling time trial. An hour before the training session each athlete was given a dose of caffeine (3 mg/kg) which was repeated 40 minutes into the training session. At the end of the time trial the cyclists followed their normal sleep routine in a sleep lab (they had slept there before to ensure 'acclimatization') and their quantity and quality of sleep were measured. Whilst the consumption of caffeine did lead to a 4 per cent improvement in time trial performance (which for elite athletes is a significant advantage), the exercise combined with the caffeine led to pronounced disruptions to a variety of aspects of the participants' sleep. It took the individuals over 50 minutes to fall asleep, which was a fivefold increase on their usual time, and they also demonstrated a 16–17 per cent reduction in total sleep time, a similar level of decrease in sleep efficiency and a 38 per cent reduction in REM sleep duration. In this study, the caffeine was consumed over 5 hours prior to bedtime, and yet there were significant negative effects on both quality and quantity of sleep, to the extent that the time taken to fall asleep (greater than 50 minutes) is sufficient to be classed as indicative of insomnia (which requires a sleep onset latency of 30 minutes or longer) (10).

As this book is aimed at the working professional, the world of elite athletes is not going to be common to most of us. However, given the effect of caffeine, over 5 hours before bedtime, on the sleep patterns of extremely fit and healthy individuals, what is the effect of caffeine on you or me? There is a large and consistent body of research demonstrating that consuming caffeine, particularly within 1 or 2 hours of bedtime (but remember the previous 5 hours period in the cyclist study), increases the time it takes to fall asleep, increases the number of times individuals wake up during the night and reduces the amount of vital deep sleep (slow wave sleep) obtained during the night, with these negative changes to sleep patterns becoming greater with increasing amounts of caffeine consumed (11). In addition, and particularly relevant to working populations, is that middle-aged adults (defined as aged 40–62 in this study) were found to be more susceptible to higher doses of caffeine (400 milligrams, which is the equivalent to four or five strong coffees) than younger adults, with a consumption of 400 milligrams of caffeine (200 milligrams 3 hours before bed and 200 milligrams 1 hour before bed) leading to the quantity of their sleep being reduced by 1.5 hours! (11). Finally, in a rather extreme study, where volunteers were kept under highly controlled conditions for 49 days (yes, you read that correctly, 49 days!), the consumption of caffeine equivalent to a double espresso 3 hours before bedtime (each night for the 49 nights) led to a 40-minute delay of their circadian melatonin rhythm. There was a physiological effect on the body with a delay in the secretion of melatonin as a result of drinking just one espresso, 3 hours before bedtime, leading to a significant increase in the time it took them to fall asleep (12). While I doubt many of you drink an espresso every night just before bed, caffeine often forms part of a habitual pattern such as an evening wind-down routine, a habit which it may be worth reviewing, particularly if you consume caffeine within 2 or 3 hours of bed.

Tips, tools and techniques to try

• Reduce caffeine consumption

Research has found that insomniacs who decreased their caffeine consumption also decreased their poor sleep nights from an average of 4.8 per week to 1.2 nights per week (13).

◦ Given the consistent message from the research on the link between caffeine and poor sleep, consider stopping eating and drinking caffeine after lunchtime. If a hot drink is part of your evening routine, switch to a non-caffeinated drink, or to decaffeinated coffee (which has only a very small amount of residual caffeine in it). Not only may this help to improve both the quality and quantity of your sleep, but it will also help to break the cyclical pattern between sleep, caffeine and daytime sleepiness.

Alcohol

From as early as the nineteenth century, researchers have been keen to understand the impact of alcohol consumption on sleep, in terms of both changes to sleep duration and to the type of sleep that individuals experience. In 1883, when Monninghof and Piesbergen observed sleep depth in their participants, they found that drinking alcohol increased the speed at which the participants fell asleep and the initial soundness of their sleep, but that they became more restless and easily disturbed later in the night (1). These observations, 130 years later, are still as relevant today as they were in 1883, and yet it is only the sleep-promoting aspects of alcohol, rather than the sleep disrupting effects, that seem to take centre stage. In fact, the sleep-promoting aspects of alcohol make it one of the most frequently used 'over the counter' sleep aids (2).

If you have ever had one or two alcoholic drinks relatively close to bedtime you will know that alcohol is a very potent somnogen. Okay, so, perhaps you haven't sat at the dining room table, drinking the second glass of wine and, whilst yawning, have commented to your partner, 'Gosh, wine really is a potent somnogen, I think I will go to bed.' You will, however, have experienced the somnogenic effects – drinking alcohol in the evening (for non-alcoholic social drinkers) reduces the time it takes you to fall asleep, and enhances the quality and quantity of your non-REM sleep (3). That is why it is seen as a very effective sleeping aid. However (there had to be a however – this is a chapter on the causes of *poor* sleep), these 'positive' effects are very short-lived because alcohol is metabolized in the body relatively quickly (4), and there are disruptions to sleep in the second half of the night, regardless of the amount of alcohol consumed (1).

In 2013, Irshaad Ebrahim, Medical Director of the London Sleep Centre, and his colleagues from the Department of Psychiatry at the University of Toronto completed an assessment of 'all known scientific studies on the impact of alcohol ingestion on nocturnal sleep in healthy volunteers' (1). Given the effects of alcohol are different in the first half of the night to the second half of the night, the researchers categorized the results into first half night findings, second half night findings and whole night findings. In addition, this comprehensive review looked at the research using low doses (1–2 standard drinks), moderate doses (2–4 standard drinks) and high doses of alcohol (more than 4 standard drinks) to see whether the effects of alcohol consumption on sleep were determined by the amount of alcohol consumed. At all dose levels, drinking alcohol reduced the amount of time it took individuals to fall asleep (the somnogen effect); however, while the somnogen effect also contributed to a reduction in the amount of time individuals spent awake (known as 'wake after sleep onset') during the first half of the night, the amount of time that they spent awake during the whole night actually increased (1). Drinking alcohol, regardless of whether this was a relatively small amount of just one or two glasses, or a larger consumption of four or more glasses, caused the participants to spend more time awake during the whole night than if they had not had anything to drink. The relatively undisturbed sleep in the first half of the night became much more disturbed in the second half, to the extent that across the whole night, the amount of awakenings was worse than a no alcohol condition – so any benefit of 'good' sleep disappeared as soon as the alcohol metabolized, and sleep became much more disrupted.

Ebrahim and his fellow researchers did find that in studies where participants had consumed a significant amount of alcohol before bed (four or more drinks), the increase in deep sleep (slow wave sleep) found for all doses of alcohol in the first half of the night also continued into the second half of the night for these heavy drinking groups (1). Drinking large volumes of alcohol did correlate with an increase in slow wave sleep throughout the night. This might sound intriguing, and perhaps you might already be using this as an excuse to have a few too many drinks next weekend – 'oh, go on then, I will have another drink because I really need to get better deep sleep and I haven't drunk quite enough yet'. Even saying this sounds a little absurd, but if you need more convincing that this is not a healthy approach to sleep, or to general well-being, consider the following two points:

1. Drinking four or more alcoholic beverages a night may improve the amount of deep sleep you gain across the night, but at what cost? Four drinks a night, every night for a week is 28 drinks. If we assume that each drink was a 175 ml glass of wine at 12 per cent ABV (alcohol by volume), that equates to 2.1 units × 28 = 58.8 units per week.[1] Given that the recommended number of units per week for both men and women in the UK is currently 14 (5), this means that in order to potentially gain some increase in deep sleep, you would need to be drinking more than three times the recommended number of units each week, every week. Of course, the

health implications of this are very serious, and if this was to continue it is likely that getting good quality sleep would pale into insignificance compared with potential physical and mental well-being concerns that may arise.

2. What do you think happens to your sleep quality if you are woken up with electric shocks frequently during the night? What about your sleep quality if you are suffering with a chronic pain condition? Obviously, neither of these situations produces the best sleep outcomes, and yet the type of electrical activity in the brain seen with these two situations is similar to that found in a study looking at the effects of alcohol consumption on healthy 18- to 21-year-olds. In this experiment, the participants were monitored in a sleep lab for two consecutive nights (plus the first night of acclimatization). On one of the experimental nights they were given an alcoholic drink one hour before lights out (vodka and orange) and on the other night they were given a placebo (orange with a vodka dipped straw so that they could not tell whether it was an alcoholic drink or not). The results showed that while there was an increase in deep sleep ('delta' electrical activity) during the first half of the night on the night the participants drank the vodka and orange compared to the night when they had the placebo, there was also an increase in 'alpha' brain activity on the alcohol night. This alpha brain activation is not typically seen in the healthy sleeping brain, and indicates sleep disruption, similar to that seen in chronic pain patients or in experimental studies where participants are woken up from sleep during the night by mild electric shocks. The

disruption was also quite significant in this study; there was a 117 per cent increase in alpha level activation compared with only a 28 per cent increase in delta activation – the increase in deep sleep quality seems to be counteracted by a much more significant increase in sleep disruption (6).

Tips, tools and techniques to try

- Increase time between alcohol consumption and bed
  Given that alcohol consumption, even at relatively small doses, can decrease the time it takes you to fall asleep, it is tempting to rely on alcohol when you are struggling with your sleep patterns. However, the decrease in the time to fall asleep and the potential increase in deep sleep in the first half of the night are contrasted with increased awakenings in the second half of the night, possibly as a result of more light sleep during this period. In addition, research has also found that dreams and nightmares more frequently occur after alcohol consumption (7), and drinking alcohol can also worsen snoring and exacerbate conditions such as obstructive sleep apnoea due to the effect of alcohol in weakening the pharyngeal dilator muscle tone (8).
  - Try to leave at least 3 hours between drinking alcohol and going to bed.

- Abstain from alcohol
  A piece of research examining the effect of alcohol given 6 hours before bedtime (at bedtime the alcohol was not detectable on a breath test) found that the 'residual' effect of

alcohol led to reduced sleep efficiency, a reduction in the total amount of sleep gained in the second half of the night, along with twice as much total wake time across the night (9).

º   If you find that your sleep quality and quantity is very disrupted by drinking alcohol, then try and abstain entirely from drinking for a period of a week or more and see if this improves your sleep patterns. The difference may not be observed straight away, so persevere.

Exercise

What do Ryan Giggs, David Beckham, Sir Chris Hoy and Jason Kenny have in common? How about Chelsea, Manchester City and Southampton Football Clubs and the British Olympic bobsleigh, BMX and rowing teams? All are elite athletes, or elite teams, and all have employed a professional sleep coach to provide advice and guidance on how to improve both the length and the quality of their sleep (1). In the world of professional sport, marginal gains are critical, and sports scientists are now turning to the field of sleep to increase competitive advantage, whether this be by supporting the athletes in their personal sleep regimes, or by creating better sleep environments such as the sleep pods installed at Manchester United Carrington training ground for players to nap between double sessions during the summer, or Manchester City Football Club's new £200 million complex which has 32 en-suite bedrooms decorated with 'sleep inducing wallpaper¹' (2).

In 2011, researchers at the Stanford Sleep Disorders Clinic at Stanford University in the United States conducted a study to look at the effect of increasing the duration of sleep in college basketball players. Rather than approaching this from a deprivation angle, and wanting to see what happens to sport performance when individuals don't get enough sleep, these researchers hoped to show that they could improve performance by increasing sleep – a glass half full rather than glass half empty approach. They took eleven college basketball players, a small sample in terms of number of participants but certainly not in terms of height (average height was 6 feet 4 inches), and asked them to gain as much sleep as they were able to during a 5 to 7-

week period (they were aiming for 10 hours' sleep per night). During this time, they were also asked to stop drinking caffeine and alcohol. Not only did players' mood, mental and general physical well-being increase as a result of gaining more sleep, but they became faster on a timed sprint, and, perhaps most fundamentally for basketball players, their shooting accuracy improved by a whopping 9 per cent (3).

Given the importance of sleep on physical and cognitive functioning, it is perhaps not surprising that good quality and quantity of sleep improves sports performance, whether you are an elite athlete or a weekly gym goer. But what about the effect of exercise on sleep? If good quality sleep of the right length can improve athletic performance, is the reverse true, can exercise itself improve sleep? The majority of studies examining this relationship have found that regular physical exercise produces significant benefits to sleep, and as a result, the American Academy of Sleep Medicine recommends exercise as a sleep hygiene measure, but not late in to the evening or night because of the possible physiological and cognitive arousal effects of exercise on the brain and body (4). This is an important point – exercise can have a very positive effect on an individual's sleep patterns, but timing of exercise is key. In addition, research has also considered not just the contribution of *when* you do the exercise, but also what *type* of exercise improves sleep quality and quantity, and how *long* you need to exercise for.

Following on from the American Academy of Sleep Medicine, the current consensus from several reviews of the research is that exercise before noon has little effect on subsequent sleep patterns; approximately 1 hour of moderate aerobic activity during the afternoon can improve the amount of deep sleep an individual gains that night, plus it has been shown to decrease the total amount of time a person wakes during the night, and that exercise in the late evening, particularly if it is high intensity, can impair sleep (5). Timing of exercise, therefore, is key, not just to whether exercise has any effect on sleep, but whether the effect is, in fact, beneficial or detrimental. For example, researchers comparing the effects of exercise at 2 pm and 8 pm found that it took participants longer to fall asleep, they woke up more times in the night and had less deep (slow wave) sleep when they exercised at 8 pm compared to 2 pm, and in addition, the 2 pm exercise group slept for longer during the night and had a better sleep efficiency (6).

In terms of the *type* of exercise that has an impact, a large review of sixty-six studies on sleep and exercise compared the effects of 'acute' and 'regular' exercise. In their analysis, the researchers defined 'acute' as less than one week of exercise, and regular exercise as equal to or more than one week of exercise, before the sleep study. Practically, the difference here is between the effects on sleep of an individual who does not exercise, but is asked to do so for the purposes of a sleep study compared to that of a person who already has a regular exercise routine. The researchers found that *both* acute and regular exercise benefited sleep, but that the effects were stronger for the regular exercise studies. Improvements in sleep, even for acute exercise, included increased duration of sleep, reduced time to fall asleep, greater sleep efficiency, more deep (slow wave) sleep and less night awakenings (7). So there really is no excuse – even if you don't exercise regularly, just starting to exercise may improve your sleep duration and quality, and if you continue your exercise regime, the effects will become stronger.

So, finally, how long do you need to exercise for? While the literature on length of exercise is not as large as the research on the type of exercise or the importance of time of day, a study that combined the results of thirty-eight pieces of research on sleep and exercise found that the length of time participants exercised for was an important variable in the subsequent impact of the exercise on sleep. Exercise of greater than 1 hour in length appears to be when the benefits to sleep are found (8), and generally, the longer the bout of exercise, the greater the benefit to subsequent sleep (7).

Tips, tools and techniques to try

- Importance of Exercise
  Even if you do not currently exercise, just 1 week of moderate exercise can improve both your sleep quality and sleep quantity including helping you to fall asleep quicker, wake up less during the night and gain more deep sleep (7).
  - Start a moderate exercise regime; you should notice the benefits that night. By continuing to exercise, and developing a regular exercise routine, the benefits to your subsequent sleep will continue to increase.

- Timing of Exercise
  According to the body of research, the most beneficial effects of exercise on sleep happen if you exercise 4–8 hours before bed (9). This allows any physiological changes that occur with exercise, such as the secretion of cortisol and endorphins and increased cardiovascular activity (such as increased heart rate) to have regulated (4), and for the cognitive arousal often

associated with exercise (one of the many benefits of regular exercise) to have reduced, so that you can relax and unwind efficiently.

- ○ When scheduling exercise, try wherever possible, to leave at least 4 hours after exercise before you go to bed. Exercise first thing in the morning is most certainly better than no exercise at all,[2] but may have only a small or no effect on your sleep, so if you are able to move this morning exercise session to lunchtime or slightly later, this may have a positive impact on your sleep.
- Duration of exercise
  - ○ Wherever possible, try and exercise for at least an hour to maximize the likely benefits to your sleep.

9

Physiological factors – shift work and jet lag

Shift work

'After a thorough review and discussion on the published scientific evidence, an expert working group, convened by the International Agency for Research on Cancer Monographs Program has concluded that shift work that involves circadian disruption is probably carcinogenic to humans' (1). As discussed in the chapter on sleep and physical health, the WHO classified shift work, where naturally occurring sleep rhythms are affected, as potentially causing cancer. For the WHO, shift work sits in the same cancer risk category (Group 2A) as nitrogen mustard, anabolic steroids and occupational exposure to petroleum refining. Given this stark statement, it is perhaps not surprising then that a very large study of nurses found a 36 per cent increased risk in breast cancer in those working shifts (2), and a study of Danish women aged between 30 and 54 years old found that those who worked at night for at least 6 months had a 50 per cent increased risk of breast cancer, even after taking into account important factors such as reproductive history and socioeconomic status (3).

But, we need to be clear – shift work per se does not cause cancer; the phrase 'circadian disruption' is critical in the WHO press release. Shift work does not cause cancer, but shift work that *affects* the circadian rhythms of an individual may ultimately result in an increased risk of developing cancer. It is not the working pattern itself, but the disruption in biological sleep processes as a result of the working pattern, that is the vital component. Some very interesting research on cancer and blind individuals may help to explain this point. Researchers have found a reduction of breast cancer risk of between 20 and 50 per cent in blind women, and a relationship between level of blindness and level of risk – the more severe the level of blindness, the lower the risk of developing breast cancer (4). While the reasons for this intriguing research are still being understood, it has been suggested that melatonin (the sleep hormone) helps protect against breast cancer as it has a potentially tumour-inhibiting effect. For blind women, the secretion of melatonin is not determined by light exposure in the way that it is for women with sight, but melatonin is still released, presumably dictated by an internal mechanism rather than external light and dark, to aid sleep. For non-blind women, light and dark is used as an external cue for the release or suppression of melatonin. At night, melatonin is released to aid sleepiness, but for those women working shifts, particularly a night shift, nocturnal artificial light suppresses the usual release of melatonin and, therefore, reduces the positive cancer-inhibiting benefits of this hormone. It is not difficult to see why prolonged shift working may lead to an increase in cancer risk, not because of the shifts themselves, but because of the physiological sleep-related consequences of the disruption in sleep cycles.

While there is no legal definition of shift work, it is generally considered to be a work schedule where at least 50 per cent of the work is to be done outside the hours of 8 am–4 pm (5), with approximately 15–20 per cent of full-time workers working alternative shifts (6). The most common of these is the early morning shift (4 am–7 am start time) (7), with the early afternoon shift starting between 2 pm and 6 pm, and the night shift starting between 6 pm and 4 am (8). While the impact of shift work is at its greatest for those on rotating night shifts (particularly fast rotations), early morning shift workers have been shown to have significantly less sleep than those who work during the day, and in fact the sleep disruption is seen as very similar to permanent night workers (9).

As we know from the first chapter in this book ('The Wake-up Call'), as humans we have two fundamental sleep drives: the linear process which is determined by how much sleep we have had (Process S) and the 24-hour circadian processes (Process C). For people who work during the day, and sleep at night, these two processes are usually in alignment (and, if not, hopefully by now this book should have convinced you of the importance of getting the two in alignment!), but for those individuals working shifts, the two become misaligned.

Remember the ball (Process C) and conveyor belt (Process S) analogy? At the start of a night shift for example, your circadian Process C (the ball) is telling you it is time to sleep (because it is dark), but you have only just woken up and are at the start of the conveyor belt, so your drive for sleep is low (Process S). Conversely, at the end of a night shift, Process C (the ball) is telling you to be wide awake because it is daylight and warm, but you have just worked a 12-hour shift and are exhausted (Process S). You are at the top of the belt ready to sleep, but the ball is at the bottom – the misalignment.

It is these types of misalignment, and the physiological disruption to circadian rhythms as a result of these, that lead to serious health and social consequences. To put this in context for those of you lucky enough to have never experienced shift work, the effect of shift work has been likened to a long-distance traveller working in San Francisco and returning to London for any rest days. Remember, this is not just a one-week business trip; shift work can be seen as the equivalent of doing this *constantly*, with the quantity of sleep being reduced by as much as 2 hours per night (or day) after a night shift (10).

For the 15–20 per cent of the working population on shift work, and, perhaps more importantly, the 4.3 per cent of the workforce (US figures) who work night shifts (8), the increased risks are not just related to cancer of course, but *all* of the cognitive and physical consequences of poor sleep we introduced in Part One of this book. These include cardiovascular disease, metabolic syndrome, obesity and increased BMI, as well as the increased risk of road traffic and workplace accidents, and social disruption. For example:

Risk of:	Increased risk level
Cardiovascular disease	40 per cent increased risk for shift workers due to disruption of circadian rhythms, disturbed social patterns and social support, stress, smoking, poor diet and lack of exercise (11).
Metabolic syndrome[1]	1.5 times higher risk among shift workers taking into account age and physical activity (12)
Obesity	Approximately 47.2 per cent of shift workers are overweight and 2.8 per cent are obese (13)

Risk of:	Increased risk level
Increased BMI	A longer exposure to shift work predicts a higher BMI (14)
Road traffic accidents	Drivers are fifty times more likely to fall asleep at the wheel at 2 am than at 10 am (15) 22 per cent of rotating shift workers had a road accident citing sleepiness as a cause compared with 7 per cent of day workers (16)
Workplace accidents	Working a night shift increases on-site accidents by 50 per cent (17)
Social consequences	Shift work increases the risk of marital separation by 7–11 per cent (18)

The research on the consequences of shift work paints a very grim picture, and the large and ever-growing body of literature on this continues to support this less than positive relationship. Jim Horne, in his book *Sleepfaring*, describes a particularly impactful piece of research where 48,000 people took part in a study over a 20-year period, during which time their health, sleep and work practices were monitored. Of the people who took part in the study, 160 of them died in a workplace accident as a result of a mistake they made, and the most important predictors of these fatal accidents were not age, education, socio-economic group, workload or overtime, but being male, reporting difficulties in sleeping and working nights (19).

It is important, however, to be pragmatic. We live in a 24-hour society, and whether we fundamentally believe or not that this is the right way to exist, we are surrounded by goods and services 'on demand'. Even if we are prepared to sacrifice our fresh bread at 2 am or our online book order at 5 am for the health of shift workers, what about keeping our homes warm and keeping our cities well lit, what about our firefighters and police officers, and what about doctors, nurses and other hospital staff, working shifts to ensure access to 24-hour medical care? Shift work allows not just access to luxury goods and services, but also to round-the-clock emergency services. Whilst it is not feasible, or even desirable to eradicate shift work, it is important to understand :

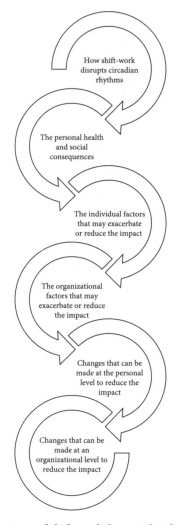

FIGURE 9.1 *The impact of shift work from individual to organization.*

For those individuals required to work shifts, a permanent shift pattern, even if this is permanent nights, may seem to be the best option, with the assumption that a regular routine can help to regulate the sleep cycle. However, first, we need to recognize the potential social consequences of permanent night shifts such as social marginalization (10), and in addition, researchers have found that only a very small minority (approximately 3 per cent) of permanent night workers show full circadian adjustment to their work schedule, and less than one-fourth adjust enough to protect against the negative cognitive and health consequences (8). It is important, therefore, to understand what can be done to help support shift workers, at both the personal level and the organizational level, to help reduce the impact of shift work on health and well-being.

Tips, tools and techniques to try

- Individual differences
  Individuals on the same shift pattern can differ quite dramatically on two particular consequences – excessive sleepiness and insomnia (9). The inability of some individuals to tolerate shift work at all has led to the development of a specific circadian rhythm disorder known as shift work sleep disorder, with the primary complaints of insomnia symptoms and/or excessive sleepiness, which cannot be explained by any other medical or mental health issue (20). Even if the effects of shift work are not at the level of a clinical diagnosis, there can still be significant individual differences. This may partly be explained by a 50 per cent genetic heritability for

vulnerability to insomnia (21), but also by the effects of age, with older workers tolerating shift work less well than younger individuals (10).

- ○ If you are responsible for the allocation of shifts, try and consider age as well as the social and personal circumstances of individuals when deciding on shift patterns.

- Napping
  Researchers have found that napping during a night shift was associated with a significant improvement in the performance speed in doctors (22), and that naps prior to the start of a night shift had a beneficial effect on alertness and performance during the shift (8). In addition, a nap during the first half of the night shift was found to increase alertness the next morning, presumably because the first half of the night, and therefore the nap, contains more slow wave sleep (23).
  - ○ If at all possible, try and have a nap before the start of a shift to reduce the 'drive for sleep', and if you feel sleepy during the first half of a night shift, this may also be a good time (if possible and safe) to take a nap.

- Choice
  Research has found that giving shift workers the opportunity to exercise some control over their working time and choice of shift pattern helped minimize the negative impact of their work schedule (24).
  - ○ If you are responsible for the allocation of shifts, discuss shift choices with individual staff. If they feel they have

some personal choice and freedom over their allocated pattern (wherever possible and practical), this may mitigate against some of the negative effects.

- Light exposure

  Given the importance of light and dark as zeitgebers (external cues to synchronize the body's circadian rhythm), it is not surprising that research has found that exposure to bright light can move the circadian rhythm. In the chapter on technology, temperature and noise, we looked at how light can *disrupt* sleep patterns, but in relation to shift work, exposure to bright light can actually *help* recalibrate the internal circadian rhythms. Exposure to bright light close to bedtime (natural bedtime) can create a 30-minute shift backwards of the biological clock (falling asleep 30 minutes later), whereas exposure to bright light approximately 2 hours before wake time can lead to a shift forwards (falling asleep 30 minutes earlier that subsequent night) (8). Conversely, the use of dark glasses, to restrict the amount of light hitting the eyes, can also be helpful for individual acclimatizing to shift work. At the end of a night shift, if you need to make a dash to the shops before you go to bed (in the bright sunlight), wearing dark glasses or goggles (it may not be the sexiest look) has been found to reduce fatigue, and, when used in combination with bright light at the appropriate times, can increase vigour and sleep duration (25).

  ○ Try and use light and dark (bright lights and dark glasses) to adjust your external environment to match your own sleep state, and to align your circadian rhythm.

- Direction and speed of rotation

  The human biological clock (circadian pacemaker) runs
  naturally at just over 24 hours. That is, without the external
  cues (zeitgebers) to bring the clock in line with the 24-hour
  day, the body would naturally run at about 24.5 hours. It is
  thought that this is the reason why research has found that
  forward-rotating shifts are less disruptive for most individuals,
  with studies showing that both sleep quantity and sleep
  quality are significantly better in forward-rotating shifts
  (8). In addition, slower rotating shifts also appear to allow a
  more effective adjustment. For example, a piece of research
  conducted in a large factory found that workers on a 21-
  day shift rotation reported a 70 per cent drop in complaints
  about shift changes, increased shift satisfaction and in general
  health, and a reduction in staff turnover, along with an
  impressive increase in manufacturing productivity (26).

  ○ Whenever you have a choice, consider slow rotating,
     forward-moving shifts.

Jet lag

In 2016, organizations across the globe reported to have spent more than $1.2 trillion on international business travel. $1.2 trillion in *one year*. This is equivalent to 1.5 per cent of the world's GDP, and this expense is growing at a rate of approximately 6.5 per cent per year, which is almost twice the rate of global economic growth (1).

This international travel comes at a further cost. A study conducted by Airbus and Kayak, the holiday company, estimated that jet lag reduced business productivity by approximately 40 per cent, resulting in 20 million lost working days per year. In addition, mistakes made at work as a result of jet lag were reported to be costing organizations in excess of £241 million in the past 12 months (2). Added to this are not just the cognitive, social and emotion and health consequences of poor sleep, but also the extra impact on cognitive performance, mood and alertness because while suffering from jet lag an individual will be working against their natural circadian rhythm (being awake when their body temperature is low[2] and trying to sleep when it is high) (3).

International business travel, whilst often sounding very glamorous, is usually anything but. Spending a large amount of time in a relatively cramped environment, with restricted food, no chance of exercise or fresh air, dehydration due to dry cabin air, the possibility of cabin hypoxia (which causes fatigue) or deep vein thrombosis (4), is not the ideal recipe for a relaxing and pleasant trip. Given you may be leaving the plane and going straight into a meeting, the impact of such flying conditions are even more important – think about the effect of poor sleep on decision-making for example. Many of these symptoms don't even require a plane journey, as a long road or rail trip can also create travel fatigue. However, once you have reached your destination and have had time to rest, travel fatigue will often disappear, especially if you increase hydration (water or fruit juice), take some roughage to eat on the journey (e.g. apples) and take a shower and brief nap on arrival at your destination (4).

Jet lag, usually occurring when three or more time zones are crossed (although some people are more susceptible than others), shares some symptoms with general travel fatigue, but there is one important difference – the effects of jet lag do not disappear after one night of good sleep, it can take many more days. While the exact length of time it takes to 'get over' jet lag varies from individual to individual, a good rule of thumb is to work on the premise that the number of days to recover is roughly equal to two-thirds the number of time zones crossed (4). For example, flying from the UK to the East Coast of the US (say, New York) crosses five time zones, and so will take approximately 3.3 days to recover, whereas a trip to Australia from the UK will take a whopping 6 days before your jet lag disappears.

Given that it is possible to create the effects of jet lag in a laboratory situation, without changes in culture, meals or temperature (4), jet lag does not require these types of travel conditions. What it does require, whether this is produced artificially in a laboratory, or naturally by crossing multiple time zones, is a body clock that has not adjusted to the time zone it finds itself in.

As discussed in more detail in other sections of the book, our daily biological, or circadian, rhythms (derived from the Latin 'circa dies' which means 'about a day') are synchronized, through external zeitgebers (time-givers), to a 24-hour solar day and without these, our body clock would naturally run at approximately 24.5 hours. Our body clock (operating 'freely' at 24.5 hours or aligned at 24 hours) produces daily rhythms in core body temperature, hormone concentrations (such as cortisol and melatonin) and the sleep/wake cycle, and these all contribute to high quality and quantity of sleep in healthy individuals. For example, as described in the chapter on technology, temperature and noise, there is a very strong relationship between core body temperature and sleep, with sleep easiest when core body temperature is falling at its most rapid or is at its lowest, and wakefulness occurs when core body temperature is rising or is at its peak. These naturally occurring rhythms, inherent in every human being, can be adjusted by external factors such as light and dark, food and exercise, but these take time – external cues do not quickly realign the body clock, which is no bad thing given that we do not want to reset our body clock every time we wake up in the middle of the night and switch on a light. However, the robustness of our internal biological clock means that when we are out of phase, it takes time to realign, hence the time it takes to recover from jet lag.

In a healthy individual, our internal (endogenous) body clock is perfectly aligned with our external environment (exogenous), so that we get tired in the evening when it is getting dark and when our body temperature is falling, we stay asleep during the night, and we wake in the morning when we stop secreting melatonin, it is light, and our core body temperature is rising (remember the ball and hill analogy in the section on shift work). Perfect internal and external synchrony for perfect sleep. In conditions of jet lag (in much the same way as happens with shift work) the internal and external components become misaligned. It may be that we have travelled from the East to the West, in which case, on arrival at our new destination, we may be ready to have an evening meal and go to bed (internal body clock programmed to go to sleep) but it is the middle of the day, the light is bright and the world (or at least the part of the world you are in) is wide awake. When we do eventually go to bed, we will often wake very early because of rising core body temperature and falling levels of melatonin produced by our unadjusted internal body clock (4). Travelling from West to East reverses the issue – we arrive at our destination still awake and ready for the rest of the day (internal body clock programmed for day time) but it is dark and everybody is heading for their beds. Just as the new day is dawning, our unadjusted body clocks prepare us for sleep!

Many of you reading this section will be very familiar with the symptoms of jet lag, and many of you more seasoned travellers will believe that you 'cope', or that you 'have got used to the effects', that you 'no longer struggle', 'have learnt to adapt' or 'just don't suffer any more'. Of course, you may have learnt some fantastic coping strategies, and you may be one of a very small minority of people that adapts more easily than others. In fact, if you are young you may well acclimatize more quickly when compared to your older colleagues, as research has consistently found that jet lag is often worse for older travellers, although the precise reason for this is still not fully understood (5). In addition, one study found that travellers with rigid sleep patterns had more jet lag symptoms than those with less rigid sleep habits (6) – so if you are a young, flexible sleeper, you may have a little more protection that the rest of us mere mortals. However, for the majority of us, being a regular traveller does not protect against the symptoms of jet lag – you do not get physiologically accustomed to it, regardless of how much you are involved in international travel, as research has shown that sleep and circadian rhythms are just as much disrupted in air crew as they are in novice flyers, and the effects can be just as significant (7). In fact, not only do the physiological effects not diminish with 'practice', long-term international travel may have an increased detrimental effect. Kwangwook Cho, working at the Medical School at the University of Bristol, was the first person to show significant changes in the brain structure of long-haul air cabin crew who had a short recovery time between transmeridian flights when compared to long-haul cabin crew who had a longer recovery time between flights. In 2000, Cho and colleagues examined the effects of repeated jet lag on cognitive abilities by comparing professional airline cabin crew[3] with ground staff at an airport. They found that not only did cabin crew have higher levels of salivary cortisol than ground crew, but that international transmeridian flying was associated with significantly raised cortisol levels rather than short-haul flights; the cortisol effect was not due to flying per se (8). Given that research has found that chronic exposure to high levels of corticosteroids (such as cortisol) in the body can lead to a reduction in cognitive functioning (9), it is perhaps of no surprise that the air crew, when compared to ground staff, were also impaired in their reaction time to cognitive tasks (8). Given these impactful findings, Cho was keen to understand whether jet lag, resulting in chronic exposure to salivary cortisol, would lead not only to reduced cognitive abilities, but also to fundamental changes in the structure of the brain, as previous studies had hypothesized that significantly high cortisol in the body over a period of time can result in hippocampal atrophy –

a reduction in the size of the hippocampus, the part of the brain critical for the consolidation of memory and learning (10).

Cho scanned the brains of twenty aircrew, each with just 5 years of flying experience. Ten of the individuals had less than 5 days of recovery between flights, crossing at least seven time zones (short recovery group), and the other ten participants had a recovery period of more than 14 days between transmeridian flights (long recovery group). The MRI brain scans showed that flight attendants from the short recovery group had significantly smaller right hippocampal volume than the long recovery group; they also had slower reaction times, and higher salivary cortisol levels. The research demonstrated that after only *five years* of long-haul flights, when there was less than a week between flights to rest and recover, not only did flight attendants have increased levels of the stress hormone cortisol, not only did they have reduced cognitive abilities in the form of reaction time, but an area of the brain, critical for memory and learning, had actually reduced in size (11)! If this wasn't enough, research has also found that female aircrew are more likely to have irregularities in their menstrual cycle (possibly due to the fluctuations in secretion of melatonin) (12), and increases in psychosis and major affective disorders have also been found in air attendants (13).

Unless you are long-haul air crew, or collecting enough frequent flyer miles to buy a small island, these dramatic effects are unlikely to be of serious concern. However, just like the fact that whilst serious sleep deprivation can make you very ill it doesn't take more than one night of poor sleep to cause some negative effects; the same is true for the effects of jet lag. Chronic jet lag, with little time for rest and recovery between long haul flights, may lead to quite significant cognitive and physiological effects, but it doesn't require this level of international travel before the effects are evident.

Whilst the cost of jet lag to industry may reach £241 million in just 1 year, there are relatively few studies outside of the lab examining the impact of jet lag on business performance. However, in the sporting world of marginal gains, where elite athletes often need to travel long distances to compete at major events, the studies are more abundant. Perhaps this is a comment on the perceived value of sport over business, perhaps a fair reflection of the vast amount of money to be won or lost in sporting events, or possibly, more pragmatically, a result of the fact that 'performance' is easier to measure in competitive sport than in business. Whatever the reason, the message is clear – rapid airline travel across multiple time zones reduces athletic performance in a wide range of sports such as basketball, baseball, American football, netball and skeleton bobsleigh.

Studies have shown that in national skeleton teams (think bobsleigh), neuromuscular control is reduced for 1 to 2 days after international travel (14), pretty critical if you are hurtling downhill at about 140 km/hr and experiencing the force of 5G's, and in baseball, those teams who had a 3-hour advantage (three less time zones crossed compared to their opponents) were found to have a winning percentage of 60.6 per cent, which was seen as more powerful than being the home team (15). In a retrospective study of six Australian National Netball competitions, it was found that teams who crossed two or more time zones to compete had the greatest performance deterioration compared to those teams that travelled across one or no time zone (16), and in American football, on Monday night football games (apparently a key night for professional American football) teams from the West Coast of the United States were favoured, regardless of where the matches were played. Such was the benefit of being from the West Coast that on games played on a Monday night, the home field advantage was removed for East Coast teams. The researchers believe that these findings were the result of circadian rhythm matches and mismatches – Monday night games begin at 9 pm, late by any standard, and past the peak time of day for muscular and cardiovascular performance.[4] For West Coast teams playing on the East Coast, their body clocks would lead them to feel it was 6 pm, a much better time for physical performance than 9 pm. In comparison, when the East Coast team travelled to the West Coast for a Monday night game, their body clocks would believe it was midnight, and therefore a poor performance was more likely (17). Finally, in basketball, the West–East performance enhancement/reduction has also been found, with teams travelling West to East scoring four points more an average than when they travelled East to West (18).

Jet lag causes symptoms such as fatigue and general tiredness, sleep disruption, loss of concentration, loss of appetite, gastrointestinal discomfort, headaches and metabolic changes (19). In addition to the general effects of poor sleep we have already covered in Part One of the book, jet lag, even for the non-professional athletes and non-air crew amongst us, can specifically cause lapses in attention and errors in cognitive performance, including distorted perceptions of time, space and distance (20).[5] Chronic jet lag can also have the same serious health effects as long-term shift work, as both create an underlying circadian disruption, and these effects include depression (21), exacerbation of some psychiatric disorders (22), increased risk of developing some forms of cancer (23) and infertility in women (24).

Tips, tools and techniques to try

- Adjustment of the body clock
  The faster the internal biological rhythms can adapt to the new time zone, the shorter the period of jet lag symptoms.
  - ○ Try to use light and dark to bring your biological (endogenous) rhythm in line with the external (exogenous) environment. For example, if it is your 'biological' night, but you are in a time zone where it is daytime, try and expose yourself to as much direct sunlight as possible. Take a walk outside (without sunglasses if possible) and avoid spending large parts of the day inside. Similarly, if it is your biological day, but it is dark outside and time for bed, then try to avoid bright light, even artificial light. Keep the lightning in your hotel room at a low level, and avoid the use of light-emitting technology before bed. The use of light and dark can even start in the airplane cabin, with use of the overhead light and window blinds (25). The following table suggests recommended times for light exposure and avoidance on the first day after a time zone transition (4). While every individual will have a slightly different sleep-wake cycle, this provides a good framework for guidance.

Time zone to the West (hour)	Bad local times for light exposure	Good local times for light exposure
3	0200–0800	1800–0000
4	0100–0700	1700–2300
5	0000–0600	1600–2200
6	2300–0500	1500–2100
7	2200–0400	1400–2000
8	2100–0300	1300–1900
9	2000–0200	1200–1800
10	1900–0100	1100–1700
11	1800–0000	1000–1600
12	1700–2300	0900–1500
13	1600–2200	0800–1400
14	1500–2100	0700–1300
Time zone to the East (hour)		
3	0000–0600	0800–1400
4	0100–0700	0900–1500
5	0200–0800	1000–1600
6	0300–0900	1100–1700
7	0400–1000	1200–1800
8	0500–1100	1300–1900
9	0600–1200	1400–2000
10	Same as 14 hours to West	
11	Same as 13 hours to West	
12	Same as 12 hours to West	

○ If it is possible to obtain, the use of melatonin supplements has been found to reduce the effect of jet lag if timed appropriately. Many reports confirm that 3–5 milligrams of melatonin, taken 2–3 hours before bed, increases sleepiness (4), and the American Academy of Sleep

Medicine has recommended the use of melatonin for jet lag (26). However, it should be noted that there have been no long-term studies on the effects of melatonin, and pregnant women and young people have been advised to avoid taking melatonin (27).

○ Try to adapt all of your external behaviour, such as eating meals, to be synchronized to your new time zone as soon as possible. Not only will this maximize the amount of time you have to resynchronize, research has found that the biological clock in the liver adapts more quickly than the central circadian pacemaker (28), and therefore, eating meals at the appropriate time may help bring the external and internal systems into alignment.

• Consider the length of stopover
Whilst adapting all of your behaviour to the new time zone as quickly as possible will maximize the amount of time you have to fully adjust, the effectiveness of this is dependent on the length of time you will be spending in the destination time zone.

○ Try not to change your patterns of behaviour if you are at your destination for less than 2 days, as full adaptation will not be possible, and you are likely to develop jet lag on the return journey too. Instead, wherever pragmatically possible, schedule meetings that coincide with your maximal alertness time for your departure zone, not your arrival time zone.

• Avoid 'banking' sleep

Creating a 'bank' of sleep may seem like a sensible way to build capacity for subsequent sleep loss, but sleeping out of synchrony with the new time zone is likely to enhance the anchoring of the internal biological rhythm to the old time zone (4).

- ○ Try not to sleep on flights, even if you are very tired, unless it coincides with night time at your destination.

Are you still awake?
The future

In 1925, Nathaniel Kleitman opened the first sleep laboratory and the science of sleep was born. From the 1920s to the present day, there have been some significant advances in our understanding of sleep, such as the first use of EEG to describe the five stages of sleep (in 1937), the discovery of REM sleep (in 1953), the location in the brain of the circadian clock (in 1972) and the publication of the first study (in rats) to show that chronic lack of sleep causes death (in 1983) (1). Yet, there is still so much we don't know. Why exactly do we sleep? Why do we get the majority of deep sleep in the first half of the night? What exact function does dreaming have?

Whilst there are still unanswered questions, never before has the appetite to answer them been so great, with cutting-edge research being published every day. For example, recent investigations are now focusing on the relationship between sleep and dementia. Researchers have found that there is a very specific link between REM sleep and dementia, with every 1 per cent reduction in REM sleep being associated with a 9 per cent increase in risk of dementia, even after factors such as vascular risk, medication use and depression symptoms are taken into account (2). In addition, studies looking at sleep processes in non-human animals are finding some exciting results which are also being related to brain disorders. Researchers at the University of Rochester reported that the brain cells of mice shrink during sleep, opening up the gaps between neurons which allow the brain to clear itself of toxic proteins (beta-amyloids). The researchers suggest that the restorative function of sleep in humans may, therefore, be as a result of the removal of this neurotoxic waste that appears to collect during wakefulness, and indeed the failure to remove this waste (which may happen with insufficient sleep) could play a role in human brain disorders (3).

Given that the sleep technology business is expected to reach $80 billion by 2020 (4), there appears to be little doubt that individuals, and organizations are now waking up to the importance of sleep. Yet, how much of this is opportunist commercialism, and how much of this is a fundamental shift away from the macho attitudes of organizations that focused on presenteeism and the long working hours culture as a badge of honour, rather than productivity, only time will tell. Certainly the signs are more positive now than they ever have been. However, given that nearly half of the US and UK adult population are not getting enough sleep (5), and given the cognitive, social, emotional and health consequences of this, there is clearly still a need for all of us to take *The Business of Sleep* seriously.

NOTES

Introduction

1   There is still quite a debate among sleep researchers as to whether, globally, we are getting any less sleep per night than our ancestors. What is of little doubt, however, is that certain subsections of the population are reporting to get significantly less than the recommended amount for their specific demographic.

2   80,300,000 hits on Google.

3   Searching on 'sleep deprivation' on the *Guinness Book of World Records* site on the internet brings up some fascinating and some very bizarre records, some of which I am not sure of the connection to sleep deprivation (including the largest home in a converted airliner, the largest insect house and the longest garbage truck ramp jump!).

4   As an employer, if you want to put this in context – research has shown that having approximately 1.5 hours less sleep a night than you need means that you are about one-third less alert the next day (13). If you have three people working for you, this is the equivalent of paying for one person to be asleep all day!

5   Considered to be the greatest German literary figure of modern times.

6   A slightly longer, but better, way to find out how much sleep you need is to take a two-week period when you are not at work, and when you are able to go to bed and wake up naturally without any distractions (yes, I know that this is almost an impossibility and this may rule out most of you from trying this!). Go to bed at the same time each night (before midnight) and wake up naturally in the morning. This means no daylight waking you up, no alarm clock and no small children poking you in the eyes. After about a week, your body will have found its natural rhythm, and you will be waking up when you have had enough sleep. For the majority of you, this will be between 7 and 9 hours.

7   'Roughly' is an important term here – research has consistently found that if individuals are provided with an environment that has no 'zeitgebers' to regulate the circadian rhythms, the natural cycle will be 24.5 hours in

length (16). Time givers such as light and dark bring this 24.5 hours cycle in line with the 24-hour clock. While this may seem of little consequence, for densely blind individuals, this can often mean they require administration of melatonin to ensure their circadian rhythms are aligned to the 24-hour day (17).

8   In 2007 the American Academy of Sleep Medicine (20) published a new manual which changed the terminology of the different stages of sleep. Many of us are familiar with stage 1 and 2 sleep (light sleep) and stage 3 and 4 sleep (deep sleep). N1 and N2 are the same as stage 1 and stage 2 light sleep, and N3 combines stage 3 and stage 4 slow wave, or deep sleep.

9   Despite huge advances in sleep research, it is still unknown why the majority of SWS occurs in the first half of the night, and the majority of REM sleep in the second half.

Chapter 4

1   To be totally honest, I haven't come across a study that has looked for this correlation – but stick with the example, it does make sense!

2   If you want to calculate your sleep efficiency – (time asleep/time in bed) × 100. You don't want 100 per cent efficiency, as this suggests you are going to bed too tired; it should take you about 10–15 minutes to fall asleep, but equally, an efficiency percentage of less than 85 per cent is normally indicative of poor sleep efficiency.

Chapter 5

1   Emotions are related to a specific cause, and are often transient, whereas moods are more general, longer lasting, and tend to be categorized as either positive or negative.

2   Hostility was also found to be a critical negative emotion affected by poor sleep in a study I conducted with a colleague at the University of Central Lancashire in the UK, with young offenders in a young offender institution (6).

Chapter 6

Temperature

1 Okay, maybe this was a lack of imagination rather than an insight into the science of sleep and temperature.

2 The proximal regions of the body follow a similar pattern of temperature change to the core, due to the lack of AVAs in the proximal areas of the body, and thus reliance on the inefficient capillary blood flow to regulate cooling.

3 The key lesson here is that Grans are always right in the end.

Noise

1 From 20 to 20,000 hertz.

2 Subjective and objective sleep effects have shown up in types of traffic noise too – researchers found that road traffic noise caused the greatest changes in objectively measured sleep quality and quantity, but that noise from trains or from planes was reported by participants as being the most disturbing (10).

Chapter 7

1 If you want to see how high your drive for sleep is - try a variation of the Multiple Sleep Latency Test, which is used to test for excessive daytime sleepiness in a variety of sleep disorders. On a day when you are able to take a daytime nap, find a quiet room and turn off the lights (so the room is dark and comfortable enough for you to fall asleep). Time how long it takes you to fall asleep. The quicker you fall asleep, the higher your drive for sleep. Insomnia patients would find this test very difficult, and although they may report feeling fatigued, their low drive for sleep would mean they would be unlikely to fall asleep at all in this situation.

Chapter 8

Alcohol

1 If you would like to calculate units of alcohol based on ABV the formula is – Strength (ABV) × Volume (ml)/1000 = Units.

Exercise

1 This is apparently light green with ever-decreasing circles printed on it!

2 Interestingly, there is a body of evidence to suggest that exercise is more likely to become habit-forming if you carry out the exercise first thing in the morning (10). It may be worth considering the benefits of exercise more holistically – if exercising in the morning means you are more likely to continue, then this may be better than changing your routine to the afternoon or early evening to improve your sleep but finding that this means you stop exercising altogether.

Chapter 9

Jet lag

1 Metabolic syndrome is defined as an individual with at least three of the following five medical conditions: abdominal obesity, elevated blood pressure, increased fasting plasma glucose levels, high serum triglycerides and low high-density lipoprotein levels (HDL).

2 Mental performance increases with rising core temperature

3 The cabin crew all crossed at least eight time zones per week, with a two- to four-day break between flights.

4 Peak physical performance has been shown in some studies to be aligned with peak core body temperature.

5 There is a very serious message here – driving while tired is dangerous, driving while jet lagged can be even more dangerous because of the potential changes to perception, judgement of distance, and of time and space.

BIBLIOGRAPHY

Introduction

(1) Dickens, C. (2008 Reprint). *The Tale of Two Cities*. Oxford: Oxford University Press.

(2) http://www.cdc.gov/features/dssleep/

(3) https://sleepfoundation.org/sleep-polls-data/other-polls/2013-international-bedroom-poll

(4) Watson, N., Safwan, M., Belenky, G., Bliwise, D., Buxton, O., Buysse, D. et al. (2015). Recommended amount of sleep for a healthy adult: A joint consensus statement of the American Academy of Sleep Medicine and Sleep Research Society. *Journal of Clinical Sleep Medicine*, 11, 591–592.

(5) Kochanek, K., Murphy, S., Xu, J. and Arias, E. (2014). Mortality in the United States, 2013. *NCHS Data Brief*, 178, 1–8.

(6) Winter, C. (2017). *The Sleep Solution: Why Your Sleep Is Broken and How to Fix It*. Scribe: Melbourne.

(7) Wagner, D., Barnes, C., Lim, V. and Ferris, D. (2012). Lost sleep and cyberloafing: Evidence from the laboratory and a daylight saving time quasi-experiment. *Journal of Applied Psychology*, 97, 1068–1076.

(8) Barnes, C., Lucianetti, L., Bhave, D. and Christian, M. (2015). You wouldn't like me when I'm sleepy: Leaders sleep, daily abusive supervision, and work unit engagement. *Academy of Management Journal*, 58, 1419–1437.

(9) Guarana, C. and Barnes, C. (2107). Lack of sleep and the development of leader-follower relationships over time. *Organizational Behavior and Human Decision Processes*, 141, 57–73.

(10) Barnes, C., Ghumman, S. and Scott, B. (2013). Sleep and organizational citizenship behaviour: The mediating role of job satisfaction. *Journal of Occupational Health Psychology*, 18, 16–26.

(11) Barnes, C., Schaubroeck, J., Huth, M. and Ghumman, S. (2011). Lack of sleep and unethical conduct. *Organizational Behavior and Human Decision Processes*, 115, 169–180.

(12) Hafner, M., Stepanek, M., Taylor, J., Troxel, W. and van Stolk, C. (2016). *Why Sleep Matters – The Economic Costs of Insufficient Sleep*. RAND Europe: Cambridge.

(13) Bonnet, M. and Arand, D. (1995). We are chronically sleep deprived. *Sleep*, 18, 908–911.

(14) https://www.brainyquote.com/quotes/quotes/j/johannwolf161315.html

(15) Hirshkowitz, M., Whiton, K., Albert, S., Alessi, C., Bruni, O., DonCarlos, L. et al. (2015). National Sleep Foundation's sleep time duration recommendations: Methodology and results summary. *Sleep Health*, 1, 40–43.

(16) Czeisler, C., Weitzman, E., Moore-Ed, M., Zimmerman, J. and Knauer, R. (1980). Human sleep: Its duration and organization depend on its circadian phase. *Science*, 210, 1264–1267.

(17) Sack, R., Brandes, R., Adam, B., Kendal, B. and Lewy, A. (2000). Entrainment of free-running circadian rhythms by melatonin in blind people. *The New England Journal of Medicine*, 343, 1070–1077.

(18) Carskadon, M. and Dement, W. (2011). Monitoring and staging human sleep. In Kryger, M., Roth, T. and Dement, W. (Eds.), *Principles and Practice of Sleep Medicine, 5th Edition*. Elsevier: St Louis.

(19) Rasch, B. and Born, J. (2013). About sleep's role in memory. *Physiological Review*, 93, 681–766.

(20) Iber, C., Ancoli-Israel, S. and Quan, S. (2007). *The AASM Manual for the Scoring of Sleep and Associated Events: Rules, Terminology and Technical Specifications*. American Academy of Sleep Medicine: Westchester.

Chapter 1

(1) Shapin, S. (2013). *The New Yorker*. October 14.

(2) Rasch, B. and Born, J. (2013). About sleep's role in memory. *Physiological Review*, 93, 681–766.

(3) Walker, M. (2009). The role of sleep in cognition and emotion. *Annals of the New York Academy of Science*, 1156, 168–197.

(4) Reber, P. (2010). What is the memory capacity of the human brain? *Scientific American*, May 1.

(5) Yoo, S., Hu, P., Gujar, N., Jolesz, F. and Walker, M. (2007). A deficit in the ability to form new human memories without sleep. *Natural Neuroscience*, 10, 385–392.

(6) Ellenbogen J., Hulbert J., Jiang Y. and Stickgold R. (2009). The sleeping brain's influence on verbal memory: Boosting resistance to interference. *PLoS One* 4, e4117.

(7) Walker, M. (2008). Cognitive consequences of sleep and sleep loss. *Sleep Medicine*, 9, S29–S34.

(8)   Walker, M. and Stickgold, R. (2006). Sleep, memory and plasticity. *Annual Review of Psychology*, 57, 139–166.

(9)   Fischer S., Hallschmid M., Elsner A. and Born J. (2002). Sleep forms memory for finger skills. *Proceedings of the National Academy of Sciences*, 99, 11987–11991.

(10) Vertes, R. (2005). Sleep is for rest, waking consciousness is for learning and memory of any kind. *Behavioral and Brain Sciences*, 28, 86–87.

Chapter 2

(1)   Boisjoly, R., Curtis, E. and Mellican, E. (1989). Roger Boisjoly and the Challenger disaster: The ethical dimensions. *Journal of Business Ethics*, 8, 217–230.

(2)   *Report of the Presidential Commission on the Space Shuttle Challenger Accident II*. US Government Printing Office: Washington, DC.

(3)   *Report of the Presidential Commission on the Space Shuttle Challenger Accident II. Appendix G-5.* US Government Printing Office: Washington, DC.

(4)   Mitler, M., Carskadon, M. and Graeber, R. (1988). Catastrophes, sleep and public policy: Consensus Report. *Sleep*, 11, 100–109.

(5)   Larsen, R. (2001). Decision making by military students under severe stress. *Military Psychology*, 13, 89–98.

(6)   Lavie, P., Wollman, M. and Pollack, I. (1986). Frequency of sleep related traffic accidents and hour of the day. *Sleep Research*, 15, 275.

(7)   Langlois, P., Smolensky, M., Hsi, B. and Weir, F. (1985). Temporal patterns of reported single-vehicle car and truck accidents in Texas, USA during 1980–1983. *Chronobiology International*, 2, 131–140.

(8)   Nelson, C., Dell'Angela, K., Jellish, W., Brown, I. and Skaredoff, M. (1995). Residents performance before and after night call as evaluated by an indicator of creative thought. *Journal of the American Osteopathic Association*, 95, 600–603.

(9)   Horne, J. (2012). Working throughout the night: Beyond 'sleepiness' – Impairments to critical decision making. *Neuroscience and Biobehavioral Reviews*, 36, 2226–2231.

(10) Harrison, Y. and Horne, J. (1999). One night of sleep loss impairs innovative thinking and flexible decision making. *Organizational Behavior and Human Decision Processes*, 78, 128–145.

(11) Culpin, V. and Russell, A. (2016). The wake-up call: The importance of sleep in organizational life. *Hult Research Report*.

(12) Pilcher, J. and Huffcutt, A. (1996). Effects of sleep deprivation on performance: A meta-analysis. *Sleep*, 19, 318–326.

(13) Horne, J. (1988). Sleep deprivation and divergent thinking ability. *Sleep*, 11, 528–536.

(14) Harrison, Y. and Horne, J. (2000). The impact of sleep deprivation on decision making: A review. *Journal of Experimental Psychology: Applied*, 6, 236–249.

(15) Baranski, J., Thompson, M., Lichacz, F., McCann, C., Gil, V., Pasto, L. and Pigeau, R. (2007). Effects of sleep loss on team decision making: Motivational loss or motivational gain? *Human Factors*, 49, 646–660.

(16) *Report of the Presidential Commission on the Space Shuttle Challenger Accident II. Appendix G-1.* US Government Printing Office: Washington, DC.

(17) Basner, M., Rubinstein, J., Fomberstein, K., Coble, M., Ecker, A., Avinash, D. and Dinges, D. (2008). Effects of night work, sleep loss and time on task on simulated threat detection performance. *Sleep*, 31, 1251–1259.

(18) Harrison, Y. and Horne, J. (1998). Sleep loss affects risk taking. *Journal of Sleep Research*, 7, 113.

(19) Bliss, E., Clark, L. and West, C. (1959). Studies of sleep deprivation: Relationship to Schizophrenia. *Archives of Neurology*, 81, 348–359.

(20) Neville, K., Bisson, R., French, J. and Boll, P. (1994). Subjective fatigue of C-141 aircrews during Operation Desert Storm. *Human Factors*, 36, 339–349.

(21) Couyoumdjian, A., Sdoia, S, Tempesta, D., Curcio, G., Rastellini, E., De Gennaro, L. and Ferrara, M. (2010). The effects of sleep and sleep deprivation on task-switching performance. *Journal of Sleep Research*, 19, 64–70.

(22) Venkatraman, V., Chuah, Y., Huettel, S. and Chee, M. (2007). Sleep deprivation elevates expectations of gains and attenuates response to losses following risky decisions. *Sleep*, 30, 603–609.

(23) Libedinsky, C., Smith, D., Teng, C., Namburi, P., Chen, V., Huettel, S. and Chee, M. (2011). Sleep deprivation biases the neural mechanisms underlying economic preferences. *Frontiers in Behavioral Neuroscience*, 5, 70.

Chapter 3

(1) Stickgold, R. and Walker, M. (2004). To sleep, perchance to gain creative insight? *Trends in Cognitive Sciences*, 8, 191–192.

(2) Portocarrero, E., Cranor, D. and Bove, V. (2011). Pillow talk: Seamless interface for dream priming recalling and playback. *Proceedings of the 4th*

International Conference on Tangible, Embedded and Embodied Interaction,
January 22–26, Portugal.

(3)   Strathern, P. (2001). *Mendeleyev's Dream: The Quest for the Elements.* St
      Martin's Press: New York.

(4)   Wagner, U., Gais, S., Halder, H., Verleger, R. and Born, J. (2004). Sleep
      inspires insight. *Nature,* 427, 352–354.

(5)   Drago, V., Foster, P., Heilman, K., Arico, D., Williamson, J., Montagna, P.
      and Ferri, R. (2011). Cyclic alternating pattern in sleep and its relationship
      to creativity. *Sleep Medicine,* 12, 361–366.

(6)   Easterbrook, J. (1959). The effect of emotion on cue utilisation and the
      organisation of behaviour. *Psychological Review,* 66, 183–201.

(7)   Cai, D., Mednick, S., Harrison, E., Kanady, J. and Mednick, S. (2009).
      REM, not incubation, improves creativity by priming associative networks.
      Proceedings of the *National Academy of Sciences,* 106, 10130–10134.

(8)   Kluger, J. (2017). How to wake up to your creativity. *Time,* April 30.

(9)   Ram-Vlasov, N., Tzischinsky, O., Green, A. and Shochat, T. (2016).
      Creativity and habitual sleep patterns among art and social sciences
      undergraduate students. *Psychology of Aesthetics, Creativity and the Arts,*
      10, 270–277.

(10) Caci, D., Robert, P., and Boyer, P. (2004). Novelty seekers and impulsive
      subjects are low in morningness. *European Psychiatry,* 19, 79–84.

(11) Francisco Diaz-Morales, J. (2007). Morning and evening types: Exploring
      their personality styles. *Personality and Individual Differences,* 43, 769–778.

(12) Claudio, L., Giuseppina, P., Mariangela, P., Massimo, C., Andrea, R.,
      Francesca, I. et al. (2016). Optic nerve dysfunction in obstructive sleep
      apnea: An electrophysiological study. *Sleep,* 39, 19–23.

(13) Ritter, S., Strick, M., Bos, M., Van Baaren, R. and Dijksterhuis, A. (2012).
      Good morning creativity: Task reactivation during sleep enhances
      beneficial effect of sleep on creative performance. *Journal of Sleep Research,*
      21, 643–647.

Chapter 4

(1)   Banks, S. and Dinges, D. (2007). Behavioral and physiological
      consequences of sleep restriction. *Journal of Clinical Sleep Medicine,* 3,
      519–528.

(2)   Geiger, S., Sabanayagam, C. and Shankar, A. (2012). The relationship
      between insufficient sleep and self-rated health in a nationally representative
      sample. *Journal of Environmental and Public Health,* 2012, 1–8.

(3) Fendrick, A., Monto, A., Nightengale, B. and Sarnes, M. (2003). The economic burden of non-influenza-related viral respiratory tract infection in the United States. *Archives of Internal Medicine*, 163, 487–494.

(4) Liu, T.-Z., Xu, C., Rota, M., Cai, H., Zhang, C., Shi, M.-J. et al. (2016) Sleep duration and risk of all-cause mortality: A flexible, non-linear meta-regression of 40 prospective cohort studies. *Sleep Medicine Reviews*, 32, 28–36.

(5) Gallicchio, L. and Kalesman, B. (2009). Sleep duration and mortality: A systematic review and meta-analysis. *Journal of Sleep Research*, 18, 148–158.

(6) Cappuccio, F., D'Elia, L., Strazzullo, P. and Miller, M. (2010). Sleep duration and all-cause mortality: A systematic review and meta-analysis of prospective studies. *Sleep*, 33, 585–592.

(7) www.nhs.uk/conditions/blood-pressure-(high)/pages/introduction.aspx

(8) Palagini, L., Bruno, R., Gemignani, A., Baglioni, C., Ghiadoni, L. and Riemann, D. (2013). Sleep loss and hypertension: A systematic review. *Current Pharmaceutical Design*, 19, 2409–2419.

(9) Tochikubo, O., Ikeda, A., Miyajima, E. and Ishii, M. (1996). Effects of insufficient sleep on blood pressure monitored by a new multibiomedical recorder. *Hypertension*, 27, 1318–1324.

(10) Gottlieb, D., Redline, S., Nietop, J., Baldwin, C., Newman, A., Resnick, H. et al. (2006). Association of usual sleep duration with hypertension: The sleep heart health study. *Sleep*, 29, 1009–1014.

(11) Calhoun, D. and Harding, S. (2010) Sleep and hypertension. *Chest*, 138, 434–443.

(12) Taheri, S., Lin, L., Austin, D., Young, T. and Mignot, E. (2004). Short sleep duration is associated with reduced leptin, elevated ghrelin and increased body mass index. *PLoS Medicine*, 1, 210–217.

(13) www.diabetes.org.uk/diabetes-the-basics/what-is-type-2-diabetes

(14) Yaggi, H., Araujo, A. and McKinlay, J. (2006). Sleep duration as a risk factor for the development of Type 2 diabetes. *Diabetes Care*, 29, 657–661.

(15) Spiegel, K., Leproult, R. and Van Cauter, E. (1999). Impact of sleep debt on metabolic and endocrine function. *Lancet*, 354, 1435–1439.

(16) www.iarc.fr/en/media-centre/pr/2007/pr180.html

(17) Institute of Medicine of the National Academies. (2012). *Building a Resilient Workforce: Opportunities for the Department of Homeland Security*. The National Academic Press: Washington, DC.

(18) Cohen, S., Doyle, W., Alper, C., Janicki-Deverts, D. and Turner, R. (2009). Sleep habits and susceptibility to the common cold. *Archives of Internal Medicine*, 169, 62–67.

Chapter 5

(1)   www.sleepeducation.blogspot.co.uk/2010/02/bill-clinton-importance-of-sleep.html

(2)   Culpin, V. and Russell, A. (2016). The wake-up call: The importance of sleep in organizational life. *Hult Research Report*.

(3)   Berry, D. and Webb, W. (1985). Mood and sleep in aging women. *Journal of Personality and Social Psychology*, 49, 1724–1727.

(4)   Pilcher, J. and Huffcut, A. (1996). Effects of sleep deprivation on performance: A meta-analysis. *Sleep*, 19, 318–326.

(5)   Dinges, D., Pack, F., Williams, K., Gillen, K., Powell, J., Ott, G. et al. (1997). Cumulative sleepiness, mood disturbance, and psychomotor vigilance performance decrements during a week of sleep restricted to 4–5 hours per night. *Sleep*, 20, 267–277.

(6)   Ireland, J. and Culpin, V. (2006). The relationship between sleeping problems, and aggression, anger and impulsivity in a population of juvenile and young offenders. *Journal of Adolescent Health*, 38, 649–655.

(7)   Scott, B. and Judge, T. (2006). Insomnia, emotions and job satisfaction: A multilevel study. *Journal of Management*, 32, 622–645.

(8)   Barnett, K. and Cooper, N. (2008). The effects of a poor night sleep on mood, cognitive, autonomic and electrophysiological measures. *Journal of Integrative Neuroscience*, 7, 405–420.

(9)   Steptoe, A., O'Donnell, K., Marmot, M. and Wardle, J. (2008). Positive affect, psychological well-being and good sleep. *Journal of Psychosomatic Research*, 64, 409–415.

(10) Kahneman, D. and Krueger, A. (2006). Developments in the measurement of subjective well-being. *Journal of Economic Perspectives*, 20, 3–24.

(11) Kahn, M., Fridenson, S., Lerer, R., Bar-Haim, Y. and Sadeh, A. (2014). Effects of one night of induced night-wakings versus sleep restriction on sustained attention and mood: A pilot study. *Sleep Medicine*, 15, 825–832.

(12) Yoo, S., Gujar, N., Hu, P., Jolesz, F. and Walker, M. (2007). The human emotional brain without sleep, a prefrontal amygdala disconnect. *Current Biology*, 17, R877–R878.

(13) Tempesta, D., Couyoumdjian, A., Curcio, G., Moroni, F., Marzano, C., De Gennaro, L. and Ferrara, M. (2010). Lack of sleep affects the evaluation of emotional stimuli. *Brain Research Bulletin*, 82, 194–108.

(14) Kilgore, W., Kahn-Greene, E., Lipizzi, E., Newman, R., Kamimori, G. and Balkim, T. (2008). Sleep deprivation reduces perceived emotional intelligence and constructive thinking skills. *Sleep Medicine*, 9, 517–526.

(15) Barsade, S. and Gibson, D. (2007). Why does affect matter in organisations? *Academy of Management Perspectives*, 21, 36–59.

(16) Lyubomirsky, S., King, L. and Diener, E. (2005). The benefits of frequent positive affect: Does happiness lead to success? *Psychological Bulletin*, 131, 803–855.

(17) Sharma, A. and Levy, M. (2003). Salespeople's affect toward customers: Why should it be important for retailers? *Journal of Business Research*, 56, 523–528.

(18) Isen, A. and Labroo, A. (2003). Some ways in which positive affect facilitates decision making and judgement. In S. Schneider and J. Shanteau (Eds.), *Emerging Perspectives on Judgement and Decision Research*. Cambridge Series on Judgement and Decision Making, Cambridge University Press: New York.

(19) Staw, B. and Barsade, S. (1993). Affect and managerial performance: A test of the sadder but wiser vs happier and smarter hypothesis. *Administrative Science Quarterly*, 38, 304–331.

(20) Amabile, T., Barsade, S., Mueller, J. and Staw, B. (2005). Affect and creativity at work. *Administrative Science Quarterly*, 50, 367–403.

(21) Madjar, N., Oldham, G. and Pratt, M. (2002). There's no place like home? The contributions of work and nonwork creativity support to employees' creative performance. *Academy of Management Journal*, 45, 757–767.

(22) Thoresen, C., Kaplan, S. and Barsky, A. (2003). The affective underpinnings of job perceptions and attitudes: A meta-analytic review and integration. *Psychological Bulletin*, 129, 914–945.

(23) Barsade, S. (2002). The ripple effect: Emotional contagion and its influence on group behaviour. *Administrative Science Quarterly*, 47, 644–675.

Chapter 6

(1) Randall, D. (2012). *Dreamland: Adventures in the Strange Science of Sleep*. Norton and Company, New York.

(2) www.theatlantic.com/health/archive/2014/05/thomas-edison-and-the-cult-of-sleep-deprivation/310824

(3) Derickson, A. (2013). *Dangerously Sleepy: Overworked Americans and the Cult of Manly Wakefulness*. University of Pennsylvania Press: Pennsylvania.

(4) https://greenbusinesslight.com/resources/lighting-lux-lumens-watts/

(5) Chang, A-M., Aeschbach, D., Duffy, J. and Czeisler, C. (2015). Evening use of light-emitting eReaders negatively affects sleep, circadian timing and next-morning alertness. *PNAS*, 112, 1232–1237.

(6)   Gradisar, M., Wolfson, A., Harvey, A., Hale, L., Rosenberg, R. and Czeisler, C. (2013). Sleep and technology use of Americans: Findings from the National Sleep Foundation's 2011 Sleep in America Poll. *Journal of Clinical Sleep Medicine*, 15, 1291–1299.

(7)   Zeiter, J., Dijk, D., Kronauer, R., Brown, E. and Czeisler, C. (2000). Sensitivity of the human circadian pacemaker to nocturnal light: Melatonin phase resetting and suppression. *Journal of Physiology*, 526, 695–702.

(8)   www.sleephealthfoundation.org.au/public-information/fact-sheets-a-z/802

(9)   Cajochen, C., Zeitzer, J., Czeisler, C. and Dijk, D. (2000). Dose-response relationship for light intensity and ocular and electroencephalographic correlates of human alertness. *Behavior and Brain Research*, 115, 75–83.

(10) Fossum, I., Nordnes, L., Storemark, S., Bjorvatn, B. and Pallesen, S. (2014). The association between use of electronic media in bed before going to sleep and insomnia symptoms, daytime sleepiness, morningness and chronotype. *Behavioral Sleep Medicine*, 12, 343–357.

(11) Suganuma, N., Kikuchi, T., Yanagi, K., Yamamura, S., Morishima, H, Adachi, H. et al. (2007). Using electronic media before sleep can curtail sleep time and result in self-perceived insufficient sleep. *Sleep and Biological Rhythms*, 5, 204–214.

(12) Lanaj, K., Johnon, R. and Barnes, C. (2014). Beginning the workday yet already depleted? Consequences of late-night smartphone use and sleep. *Organizational Behavior and Human Decision Processes*, 124, 11–23.

(13) Stepanski, E. and Wyatt, J. (2003). Use of sleep hygiene in the treatment of insomnia. *Sleep Medicine Reviews*, 7, 215–225.

(14) Thomee, S., Dellve, L., Harenstam, A. and Hagberg, M. (2010). Perceived connections between information and communication technology use and mental symptoms among young adults – A qualitative study. *BMC Public Health*, 10, 66.

(15) Hauri, P. and Fisher, J. (1986). Persistent psychophysiological (learned) insomnia. *Sleep*, 9, 38–53.

(16) Cain, N. and Gradisar, M. (2010). Electronic media use and sleep in school-aged children and adolescents: A review. *Sleep Medicine*, 11, 735–742.

Temperature

(1)   www.sciencing.com/cold-make-sleepy-23965.html/

(2)   Okamoto-Mizuno, K. and Mizuno, K. (2012). Effects of thermal
      environment on sleep and circadian rhythm. *Journal of Physiological
      Anthropology*, 31, 14.

(3)   Aschoff, J. and Heise, A. (1972). Thermal conductance in man: Its
      dependence on time of day and of ambient temperature. In Itoh, S., Ogata,
      K. and Yoshimura, H. (Eds.), *Advances in Climate Physiology*. Igako Shoin:
      Tokyo.

(4)   Krauchi, K. (2006). The human sleep-wake cycle reconsidered from a
      thermoregulatory point of view. *Physiology and Behavior*, 90, 236–245.

(5)   Van Someren, E. (2000). More than a marker: Interaction between
      circadian regulation of temperature and sleep, age-related changes and
      treatment possibilities. *Chronobiology International*, 17, 313–354.

(6)   Campbell, S. and Broughton. R. (1994). Rapid decline in body
      temperature before sleep: Fluffing the physiological pillow? *Chronobiology
      International*, 11, 126–131.

(7)   Lack, L. and Lushington, K. (1996). The rhythms of human sleep
      propensity and core body temperature. *Journal of Sleep Research*, 5, 1–11.

(8)   Krauchi, K., Cajochen, C. and Wirz-Justice, A. (1998). Circadian and
      homeostatic regulation of core body temperature and alertness in humans:
      What is the role of melatonin? In Honma, K. and Honma, S. (Eds.),
      Circadian Clocks and Entrainment, Vol 7. Hokkaido University Press:
      Sapporo.

(9)   Krauchi, K., Werth, E., Wuest, D., Renz, C. and Wirz-Justice, A.
      (1999). Interaction of melatonin with core body cooling: Sleepiness is
      primarily associated with heat loss and not with a decrease in core body
      temperature. *Sleep*, 22, S285–S286.

(10) Velluti, R. (1997). Interactions between sleep and sensory physiology.
      Journal of Sleep Research, 6, 61–77.

(11) Raymann, R., Swaab, D. and Van Someren, E. (2007). Skin temperature
      and sleep-onset latency: Changes with age and insomnia. *Physiology and
      Behavior*, 90, 257–266.

(12) Fletcher, A., van den Heuvel, C., and Dawson, D. (1999). Sleeping with an
      electric blanket: Effects on core temperature, sleep and melatonin in young
      adults. *Sleep*, 22, 313–318.

(13) Raymann, R., Swaab, D. and Van Someren, E. (2008). Skin deep: Enhanced
      sleep depth by cutaneous temperature manipulation. *Brain*, 131, 500–513.

(14) Okamoto, K., Iizuka, S. and Okudaira, N. (1997). The effects of air
      mattress upon sleep and bed climate. *Applied Human Science*, 16, 97–102.

(15) Libert, J., Nisi, J., Fukuda, H., Muzet, A., Ehrhart, J. and Amoros, C.
      (1988). Effects of continuous heat exposure on sleep, thermoregulation,
      melatonin and microclimate. *Journal of Thermal Biology*, 29, 31–36.

(16) Muzet, A., Libert, J. and Candas, V. (1984). Ambient temperature and human sleep. *Experientia*, 40, 425–429.

(17) Okamoto-Mizuno, K., Tsuzuki, K., Mizuno, K. and Ohshiro, Y. (2009). Effects of low ambient temperature on heart rate variability during sleep in humans. *European Journal of Applied Physiology*, 105, 191–197.

Noise

(1) Hammer, M., Swinburn, T. and Neitzel, R. (2014). Environmental noise pollution in the United States: developing an effective public health response. *Environmental Health Perspectives*, 122, 115–119.

(2) www.euro.who.int/_data/assets/pdf_file/0008/136466/e94888.pdf

(3) http://webarchive.nationalarchives.gov.uk/20100716121707/http://www.hpa.org.uk/web/HPAwebFile/HPAweb_C/1246433634856

(4) http://www.industrialnoisecontrol.com/comparative-noise-examples.htm

(5) Haralabidis, A., Dimakopoulou, K., Vigna-Taglianti, F., Giampaolo, M., Borgini, A., Dudley, M. et al. (2008). Acute effects of night-time noise exposure on blood pressure in populations living near airports. *European Heart Journal*, 29, 658–664.

(6) Jarup, L., Babisch, W., Houthuijs, D., Pershagen, G., Katsouyanni, K., Cadum, E. et al. (2008). Hypertension and exposure to noise near airports: The HYENA study. *Environmental Health Perspectives*, 116, 329–333.

(7) European Environment Agency (2003). *Europe's Environment: The Third Assessment*. EEA: Copenhagen.

(8) Muzet, A. (2007). Environmental noise, sleep and health. *Sleep Medicine Reviews*, 11, 135–142.

(9) Frei, P., Mohler, E. and Roosli, M. (2014). Effect of nocturnal road traffic noise exposure and annoyance on objective and subjective sleep quality. *International Journal of Hygiene and Environmental Health*, 217, 188–195.

(10) Basner, M., Griefahn, B., and Hume, K. (2010). Comment on: The state of the art of predicting sleep disturbances in field settings. *Noise and Health*, 12, 283–284.

(11) Ohrstrom, E. (1993). Research on noise since 1988: Present state. In Vallet, M. (Ed.), *Proceedings of Noise and Man*. INRETS: Nice.

(12) Oswald, I., Taylor, A. and Treisman, M. (1960). Discrimination responses to stimulation during human sleep. *Brain*, 83, 440–453.

(13) Carter, N. (1996). Transportation noise, sleep and possible after-effects. *Environment International*, 22, 105–116.

(14) Maschike, C. (1998). Noise-induced sleep disturbance, stress reactions and health effects. In Prasher, D. and Luxon, L. (Eds.). *Protection against Noise. Volume 1: Biological Effects.* Whurr Publishers for the Institute of Laryngology and Otology: London.

(15) Maschke, C., Harder, J., Ising, H., and Hecht, K. (2002). Stress hormone changes in persons exposed to simulated night noise. *Noise and Health*, 5, 35.

(16) Smith, A. (1990). Noise, performance efficiency and safety. *International Archives of Occupational and Environmental Health*, 62, 1–5.

(17) Wilkinson, R. and Cambel, L. (1984). Effects of traffic noise on quality of sleep: Assessment by EEG, subjective report or performance next day. *Journal of the Acoustic Society of America*, 75, 468–475.

(18) World Health Organisation (2000). Noise and health. *Health and Environment*, 36.

(19) Lercher, P., Widmann, U. and Kofler, W. (2000). Transportation noise and blood pressure: The importance of modifying factors. In Cassereau, D. (Ed.), *Internoise*. Societe Francaise d'Acoustique: Nice.

(20) Kuwano, S., Mizunami, T., Namba, S. and Morinaga, M. (2002). The effect of different kinds of noise on the quality of sleep under the controlled conditions. *Sound Vibrations*, 277, 445–452.

Chapter 7

(1) Ohayon, M. (2002). Epidemiology of insomnia: What we know and what we still need to learn. *Sleep Medicine Reviews*, 6, 97–111.

(2) Edinger, J., Bonnet, M., Bootzin, R., Doghramji, K., Dorsey, C., Espie, C. et al. (2004). Derivation of research diagnostic criteria for insomnia: Report of an American Academy of Sleep Medicine Work Group. *Sleep*, 27, 1567–1588.

(3) Lundh, L. and Broman, J. (2000). Insomnia as an interaction between sleep-interfering and sleep-interrupting processes. *Journal of Psychosomatic Research*, 49, 299–310.

(4) Lichstein, K. and Rosenthal, T. (1980). Insomniacs perceptions of cognitive versus somatic determinants of sleep disturbance. *Journal of Abnormal Psychology*, 89, 105–107.

(5) Harvey, A. (2003). The attempted suppression of presleep cognitive activity in insomnia. *Cognitive Therapy and Research*, 27, 593–602.

(6)   Harvey, A. and Payne, S. (2002). The management of unwanted pre-sleep thoughts in insomnia: Distraction with imagery versus general distraction. *Behavior Research and Therapy*, 40, 267–277.

(7)   Watts, F., Coyle, P. and East, M. (1994). The contribution of worry to insomnia. *British Journal of Clinical Psychology*, 33, 211–220.

(8)   Wicklow, A. and Espie, C. (2000). Intrusive thoughts and their relationship to actigraphic measurement of sleep: Towards a cognitive model of insomnia. *Behavior Research and Therapy*, 38, 679–693.

(9)   Tang, N., Schmidt, D. and Harvey, A. (2007). Sleeping with the enemy: Clock monitoring in the maintenance of insomnia. *Journal of Behavior Therapy and Experimental Psychiatry*, 38, 40–55.

(10) Shapiro, S., Bootzin, R., Figueredo, A., Lopez, A. and Schwartz, G. (2003). The efficacy of mindfulness-based stress reduction in the treatment of sleep disturbance in women with breast cancer: An exploratory study. *Journal of Psychosomatic Research*, 54, 85–91.

(11) Carlson, L. and Garland, S. (2005). Impact of mindfulness-based stress reduction (MBSR) on sleep, mood, stress and fatigue symptoms in cancer outpatients. *International Journal of Behavioral Medicine*, 12, 278–285.

(12) Ong, J., Ulmer, C. and Manber, R. (2012). Improving sleep with mindfulness and acceptance: A metacognitive model of insomnia. *Behavior Research Therapy*, 50, 651–660.

(13) Gross, C., Kreitzer, M., Reilly-Spong, M., Wall, M., Winbush, N. and Patterson, R. (2011). Mindfulness-based stress reduction versus pharmacotherapy for chronic primary insomnia: A randomised controlled clinical trial. *Explore*, 7, 76–87.

(14) Nelson, J. and Harvey, A. (2002). The differential functions of imagery and verbal thought in insomnia. *Journal of Abnormal Psychology*, 111, 665–669.

(15) Ciarocco, N., Vohs, K. and Baumester, R. (2010). Some good news about rumination: Task-focused thinking after failure facilitates performance improvement. *Journal of Social and Clinical Psychology*, 29, 1057–1073.

Chapter 8

(1)   Armstrong, L., Pumerantz, A., Roti, M., Judelson, D., Watson, G., Dias, J. et al. (2005). Fluid, electrolyte and renal indices of hydration during 11 days of controlled caffeine consumption. *International Journal of Sports Nutrition, Exercise and Metabolism*, 15, 252–265.

(2)   Roehrs, T. and Roth, T. (2008). Caffeine: Sleep and daytime sleepiness.
      Sleep Medicine Reviews, 12, 153–162.
(3)   Somogyi, L. (2010). Caffeine intake by the US population. Prepared for the
      Food and Drug Administration, Oakridge National Laboratory.
(4)   www.britishcoffeeassociation.org/about_coffee/coffee_facts/
(5)   Ballas, C. and Dinges, D. (2009). Modafini, Amphetamines and Caffeine.
      In Stickgold, R. and Walker, M. (Eds.), *The Neuroscience of Sleep*. Elsevier:
      Amsterdam.
(6)   Ohayon, M., Malijai, C., Pierre, P., Guilleminault, C. and Priest, R. (1997).
      How sleep and mental disorders are related to complaints of daytime
      sleepiness. *Archives of Internal Medicine*, 157, 2645–2652.
(7)   Wesensten, M. (2011). Pharmacologic Management of Performance
      Deficits Resulting in Sleep Loss and Circadian Desynchrony. In Krygor,
      M., Roth, T. and Dement, W. (Eds.) *Principles and Practice of Sleep
      Medicine*. Elsevier: St Louis, US.
(8)   Koppelstaetter, F., Poeppel, T., Siedentopf, C., Ischebeck, M., Verius, I. and
      Haala, F. et al. (2008). Does caffeine modulate verbal working memory
      processes? An fMRI study. *Neuroimage*, 39, 492–499.
(9)   Cook, C., Crewther, B., Kilduff, L., Drawer, S. and Gaviglio, C. (2011).
      Skill execution and sleep deprivation: Effects of acute caffeine or creatine
      supplementation – A randomised placebo-controlled trial. *Journal of the
      International Society of Sports Nutrition*, 8, 2.
(10) Miller, B., O'Connor, H., Orr, R., Ruell, P., Cheng, H. and Chow, C. (2014).
      Combined caffeine and carbohydrate ingestion: Effects on nocturnal
      sleep and exercise performance in athletes. *European Journal of Applied
      Physiology*, 114, 2529–2537.
(11) Robillard, R., Bouchard, M., Cartier, A., Nicolau, L. and Carrier, J. (2015).
      Sleep is more sensitive to high doses of caffeine in the middle years of life.
      Journal of Psychopharmacology, 29, 688–697.
(12) Burke, T., Markwald, R., McHill, A., Chinoy, E., Snider, J., Bessman, S.
      et al. (2015). Effects of caffeine on the human circadian clock in vivo and
      in vitro. *Science Translation Medicine*, 7, 305ra146.
(13) Edelstein, B., Keaton-Bradsted, C. and Burg, M. (1984). Effects of caffeine
      withdrawal on nocturnal enuresis, insomnia and behaviour restraints.
      Journal of Clinical Psychology, 52, 857–862.

Alcohol

(1) Ebrahim, I., Shapiro, C., Williams, A. and Fenwick, P. (2013). Alcohol and sleep: Effects on normal sleep. *Alcoholism: Clinical and Experimental Research*, 37, 539–549.

(2) Johnson, E., Roehrs, T., Roth, T. and Breslau, N. (1998). Epidemiology of alcohol and medication as aids to sleep in early adulthood. *Sleep*, 21, 178–186.

(3) Thakkar, M., Sharma, R. and Sahota, P. (2015). Alcohol disrupts sleep homeostasis. *Alcohol*, 49, 299–310.

(4) Madsen, B. and Rossi, L. (1980). Sleep and Michaelis-Menten elimination of ethanol. *Clinical Pharmacology Therapy*, 27, 114–119.

(5) www.nhs.uk/Livewell/alcohol/Pages/alcohol-units.aspx

(6) Chan, J., Trinder, J., Colrain, I. and Nicholas, C. (2015). The acute effects of alcohol on sleep electroencephalogram power spectra in late adolescence. *Alcoholism: Clinical and Experimental Research*, 39, 291–299.

(7) Rundell, O., Lester, B., Griffiths, W. and Williams, H. (1972). Alcohol and sleep in young adults. *Psychopharmacologia*, 26, 201–218.

(8) Teofilo, L. (2008). *Medication and Their Effects on Sleep: Sleep Medicine, Essential and Review*. New York: Oxford University Press.

(9) Landolt, H., Roth, C., Dijk, D. and Borbely, A. (1996). Late afternoon ethanol intake affects nocturnal sleep and the sleep EEG in middle-aged man. *Journal of Clinical Psychopharmacology*, 16, 428–436.

Exercise

(1) Littlehales, N. (2016). *Sleep*. Penguin Random House: United Kingdom.

(2) www.bbc.co.uk/sport/football/32276547

(3) Mah, C., Mah, K., Kezirian, E. and Dement, W. (2011). The effects of sleep extension on the athletic performance of collegiate basketball players. *Sleep*, 34, 943–950.

(4) Akerstedt, T. (2006). Psychosocial stress and impaired sleep. *Scandinavian Journal of Work and Environmental Health*, 32, 493–501.

(5) Miura, A., Myouken, S., Yamada, M., Fujihara, C., Miura, K., Kashima, H. et al. (2016). Effects of aerobic exercise in early evening on the following nocturnal sleep and its haemodynamic response. *Research in Sports Medicine*, 24, 16–29.

Souissi, M., Chtourou, H., Zrane, A., Cheikh, R., Dogui, M., Tabka, Z. and Souissi, N. (2012). Effect of time of day of aerobic maximal exercise on the sleep quality of trained subjects. *Biological Rhythm Research*, 43, 323–330.

(7)   Kredlow, M, Capozzoli, M., Hearon, B., Calkins, A. and Otto, M. (2015). The effects of physical activity on sleep: A meta-analytic review. *Journal of Behavioral Medicine*, 38, 427–449.

(8)   Youngstedt, S., O'Connor, P. and Dishman, R. (1997). The effects of acute exercise on sleep: A quantitative synthesis. *Sleep*, 20, 203–214.

(9)   Alley, J., Mazzochi, J., Smith, C., Morris, D. and Collier, S. (2015). Effects of resistance exercise timing on sleep architecture and nocturnal blood pressure. *Journal of Strength and Conditioning Research*, 39, 1378–1385.

(10) http://www.webmd.com/fitness-exercise/features/whats-the-best-time-to-exercise#1

Chapter 9

(1)   www.iarc.fr/en/media-centre/pr/2007/pr180.html

(2)   Davis, S., Mirick, D. and Stevens, R. (2001). Night shift work, light at night, and risk of breast cancer. *Journal of the National Cancer Institute*, 93, 1557–1562.

(3)   Hansen, J. (2001). Increased breast cancer risk amongst women who work predominantly at night. *Epidemiology*, 12, 74–77.

(4)   Feychting, M., Osterlund, B. and Ahlbom, A. (1998). Reduced cancer incidence amongst the blind. *Epidemiology*, 9, 490–494.

(5)   Hedges, J. and Sekscenski, E. (1979). Workers on late shifts in a changing economy. *Monthly Labor Review*, 10, 431–436.

(6)   Beers, T. (2000). Flexible schedules and shift work: Replacing the 9–5 workday? *Monthly Labor Review*, 123, 33–40.

(7)   American Academy of Sleep Medicine. (2014). *The International Classification of Sleep Disorders: Diagnostic and Coding Manual*. American Academy of Sleep Medicine: Darien, Illinois, US.

(8)   Cheng, P. and Drake, C. (2016). Shift work and work performance. In Barling, J., Barnes, C., Carleton, E. and Wagner, D. (Eds.), *Work and Sleep*. Oxford University Press: Oxford, UK.

(9)   Drake, C. and Wright, K. (2011). Shift work, shift-work disorder and jet lag. In Kryger, M., Roth, T. and Dement, W. (Eds.), *Principles and Practice of Sleep Medicine*. Elsevier: St Louis, US.

(10) Harrington, J. (2001). Health effects of shift work and extended hours of work. *Occupational Health Medicine*, 58, 68–72.

(11) Boggild, H. and Knuttson, A. (1999). Shift work, risk factors and cardiovascular disease. *Scandinavian Journal of Work and Environmental Health*, 25, 85–99.

(12) Sookoian, S., Gemma, C., Fernandez Gianotti, T., Burgueno, A., Alvarez, A., Gonzalez, C. and Pirola, C. (2007). Effects of rotating shift work on biomarkers of metabolic syndrome and inflammation. *Journal of Internal Medicine*, 261, 285–292.

(13) Antunes, L., Levandovski, R., Dantas, G., Caumo, W. and Hidalgo, M. (2010). Obesity and shift work: Chronobiological aspects. *Nutrition Research Review*, 23, 155–168.

(14) Parkes, K. (2002). Shift work and age as interactive predictors of body mass index among offshore workers. *Scandinavian Journal of Work and Environmental Health*, 28, 64–71.

(15) Horne, J. and Reyner, L. (1995). Sleep related vehicle accidents. *British Medical Journal*, 310, 565–567.

(16) Richardson, G., Miner, J. and Czeisler, C. (1989). Impaired driving performance in shiftworkers: The role of the circadian system in a multifactorial model. *Alcohol, Drugs and Driving*, 5–6, 265–273.

(17) Smith, L., Folkard, S. and Poole, C. (1994). Increased injuries on night shift. *The Lancet*, 344, 1137–1139.

(18) White, L. and Keith, B. (1990). The effect of shift work on the quality and stability of marital relations. *Journal of Marriage and the Family*, 52, 453–462.

(19) Horne, J. (2006). *Sleepfaring*. Oxford, UK: Oxford University Press.

(20) Vallieres, A. and Bastille-Denis, E. (2012). Circadian rhythm disorders II. In Morin, C. and Espie, C. (Eds.), *The Oxford Handbook of Sleep and Sleep Disorders*. Oxford, UK: Oxford University Press.

(21) Watson, N., Goldberg, J., Arguelles, L. and Buchwald, D. (2006). Genetic and environmental influences on insomnia, daytime sleepiness and obesity in twins. *Sleep*, 29, 645–649.

(22) Tempesta, D., Cipolli, C., Desideri, G., De Gennaro, L. and Ferrara, M. (2013). Can taking a nap during a night shift counteract the impairment of executive skills in residents? *Medical Education*, 47, 1013–1021.

(23) Sallinen, M., Harma, M., Akerstedt, T., Rosa, R., and Lillqvist, O. (1998). Promoting alertness with a short nap during a night shift. *Journal of Sleep Research*, 7, 240–247.

(24) Smith, P., Wright, B., Mackey, R., Milsop, H. and Yates, S. (1988). Change from slowly rotating 8-hour shifts to rapidly rotating 8-hour and 12-hour shifts using participative shift roster design. *Scandinavian Journal of Work and Environmental Health*, 24, 55–61.

(25) Eastman, C., Stewart, K., Mahoney, M., Liu, L. and Fogg, L. (1994). Dark goggles and bright light improve circadian rhythm adaptation to night-shift work. *Sleep*, 17, 535–543.

(26) Czeisler, C., Moore-Ede, M. and Coleman, R. (1982). Rotating shift work schedules that disrupt sleep are improved by applying circadian principles. *Science*, 217, 460–463.

Jet lag

(1) www.project-syndicate.org/commentary/why-travel-for-business-by-ricardo-hausmann-2016-01?barrier=accessreg

(2) www.kayak.co.uk/news/jet-lag-costs-brits/

(3) Waterhouse, J., Minors, D., Akerstedt, T., Reilly, T. and Atkinson, G. (2001). Rhythms of human performance. In Takahashi, J., Turek, F. and Moore, R. (Eds.), *Handbook of Behavioral Neurobiology: Circadian Clocks*. Kluwer Academic: New York.

(4) Waterhouse, J., Reilly, T., Atkinson, G. and Edwards, B. (2007). Jet lag: Trends and coping strategies. *Lancet*, 369, 1117–1129.

(5) Monk, T. (2005). Aging human circadian rhythms: Conventional wisdom may not always be right. *Journal of Biological Rhythms*, 20, 366–374.

(6) Flower, D., Irvine, D. and Folkard, S. (2003). Perception and predictability of travel fatigue after long-haul flights: A retrospective study. *Aviation Space and Environmental Medicine*, 74, 173–179.

(7) Samel, A., Wegman, H. and Vejvoda, M. (1995). Jet lag and sleepiness in air crew. *Journal of Sleep Research*, 4, 30–36.

(8) Cho, K., Ennaceur, A., Cole, J. and Suh, C. (2000). Chronic jet lag produces cognitive deficits. *The Journal of Neuroscience*, 20, 1–5.

(9) McEwen, B. and Sapolsky, R. (1995). Stress and cognitive function. *Current Opinion in Neurobiology*, 5, 205–216.

(10) Newcomber, J., Selke, G., Melson, A., Hershey, T., Craft, S., Richards, K. and Alderson, A. (1999). Decreased memory performance in healthy humans induced by stress level cortisol treatment. *Archives of General Psychiatry*, 56, 527–533.

(11) Cho, K. (2001). Chronic jet lag produces temporal lobe atrophy and spatial cognitive deficits. *Nature Neuroscience*, 4, 567–568.

(12) Grajewski, B., Nguyen, M., Whelan, E., Cole, R. and Hein, M. (2003). Measuring and identifying large-study metrics for circadian rhythm disruption in female flight attendants. *Scandinavian Journal of Work and Environmental Health*, 29, 337–346.

(13) Katz, G., Knobler, H., Laibel, Z., Strauss, Z. and Durst, R. (2002). Time zone change and major psychiatric morbidity: The results of a 6 year study in Jerusalem. *Comprehensive Psychiatry*, 43, 37–40.

(14) Chapman, D., Bullock, N., Ross, A., Rosemond, D. and Martin, D. (2011). Detrimental effects of west to east transmeridian flight on jump performance. *European Journal of Applied Physiology*, 112, 1663–1669.

(15) Winter, W., Hammond, W., Green, N., Zhang, Z. and Bliwise, D. (2009). Measuring circadian advantage in major league baseball: A 10-year retrospective study. *International Journal of Sports Physiology Performance*, 4, 394–401.

(16) Bishop, D. (2004). The effects of travel on team performance in the Australian national netball competition. *Journal of Science and Medicine in Sport*, 7, 118–122.

(17) Smith, R., Guilleminault, C. and Efron, B. (1996). Peak athletic performance time and circadian advantage in professional athletes. *Sleep Research*, 25, 573.

(18) Steenland, K. and Deddens, J. (1997). Effect of travel and rest on performance of professional basketball players. *Sleep*, 20, 366–369.

(19) Waterhouse, J., Nevill, A., Finnegan, J., Williams, P., Edwards, B., Kao, S. and Reilly, T. (2005). Further assessment of the relationship between jet lag and some of its symptoms. *Chronobiology International*, 22, 121–136.

(20) Manfredini, R., Manfredini, F., Fersini, C. and Conconi, F. (1998). Circadian rhythms, athletic performance and jet lag. *British Journal of Sports Medicine*, 32, 101–106.

(21) Kennaway, D. (2010). Clock genes at the heart of depression. *Journal of Psychopharmacology*, 24, 5–14.

(22) Katz, G., Durst, R., Zislin, Y., Barel, Y. and Knobler, H. (2001). Psychiatric aspects of jet lag: Review and hypothesis. *Medical Hypotheses*, 56, 20–23.

(23) Davis, S. and Mirick, D. (2006). Circadian disruption, shift work and the risk of cancer: A summary of the evidence and studies in Seattle. *Cancer Causes Control*, 17, 539–545.

(24) Mahoney, M. (2010). Shift work, jet lag and female reproduction. *International Journal of Endocrinology*, 2010, 813764.

(25) Arendt, J. (2009). Managing jet lag: Some of the problems and possible new solutions. *Sleep Medicine Reviews*, 13, 249–256.

(26) Morgenthaler, T., Lee-Chiong, T., Alessi, C., Friedman, L., Aurora, R., Boechlecke, B. et al. (2007). Practice parameters for the clinical evaluation and treatment of circadian rhythm sleep disorders. An American Academy of Sleep Medicine Report. *Sleep*, 30, 1445–1459.

27) Sanders, D., Chatuvedi, A. and Hordinsky, J. (1999). Melatonin: Aeromedical toxipharmacological and analytical aspects. *Journal of Applied Toxicology*, 23, 159–167.

(28) Stokkan, K., Yamazaki, S., Tei, H., Sakaki, Y. and Menaker, M. (2001). Entrainment of the circadian clock in the liver by feeding. *Science*, 291, 490–493.

Are you still awake? The future

(1) http://healthysleep.med.harvard.edu/interactive/timeline

(2) Pase, M., Himali, J., Grima, N., Beiser, A., Satizabal, C., Aparicio, H. et al. (2017). Sleep architecture and the risk of incident dementia in the community. *Neurology*, 89, 1028–1034.

(3) Xie, L., Kang, H., Xu, Q., Chen, M., Liao, Y., Thiyagarajan M. et al. (2013). Sleep drives metabolite clearance from the adult human brain. *Science*, 342, 373–377.

(4) https://sleepjunkies.com/blog/ces-2017-sleep-tech-roundup/

(5) https://sleepfoundation.org/sleep-polls-data/other-polls/2013-international-bedroom-poll

INDEX